PAPUA NEW GUINEA

Language

Grade 7

Teacher Resource Book

Susan Baing

OXFORD

Contents

Overview

Introduction

This Teacher Resource Book is for teachers to use with the *Language for Grade 7, Outcomes Edition,* Student Book. It will help teachers implement the *Language Grade 7 Syllabus 2003 for Upper Primary Students* by providing teachers with:

- information for planning a school-based program,
- a selection of teaching and learning strategies,
- a range of planning and assessment techniques, and
- ways to extend and develop content and student practice from the Student Book.

Key features of the Student Book

The Student Book is designed to help students achieve the outcomes given in the syllabus. Students will find models, examples and exercises to help them with the knowledge, skills, processes and attitudes as outlined in the syllabus. Speaking and listening, reading and writing skills are integrated. Students will find meaningful contexts to:

- use language effectively,
- increase their knowledge of language, and
- understand how language works.

The content of the Student Book:

- supports the *Language Grade 7 Syllabus 2003* by following the sequence of strands and sub-strands, while providing integration between strands and sub-strands,
- contains references to the *Upper Primary Language Syllabus* at the beginning of each chapter to show the clear relationship between the Student Book and the syllabus,
- provides four chapters for each of the strands of speaking and listening, reading, and writing,
- covers the sub-strands of production, skills and strategies, context and text, and critical literacy,
- provides topics and learning approaches that directly support the achievement of syllabus outcomes,
- includes a wide range of models, examples, exercises and activities that are student centred and provide a context for whole language learning,
- is presented in language appropriate for Grade 7 language learning,
- provides models and examples from Papua New Guinea that follow syllabus guidelines (*our way of life: cultural, multicultural, ethical, moral and showing values; and integrated human development: the right to healthy living, citizenship, sustainability*),
- uses language that is gender sensitive and includes positive gender roles,
- uses illustrations to help students understand the text and to stimulate their imaginations, and
- allows students and teachers to supplement materials with other appropriate models and examples in English, Tok Pisin or vernacular languages.

Key features of the Teacher Resource Book

Each chapter contains the following sections:

- about this strand (the role of the strand in a language program),
- key words (major words that students and teachers will be using throughout the chapter),
- links to other main subjects in the curriculum,
- possible assessment tasks (suitable to assess the skills learnt for the strand), and
- teacher information (added information for teachers in terms of specific content).

The Teacher Resource Book is designed to help teachers use the Student Book to successfully implement the *Upper Primary Language Syllabus for Grade 7*. Key topics are:

- learning and teaching strategies,
- planning suggestions and checklists,
- assessment procedures and checklists,
- assessment activities, and
- suggestions about how to further develop topics and integrate speaking and listening, reading and writing skills.

How to use the Teacher Resource Book

Learning outcomes

Outcomes-based education is used to identify and monitor progress in student learning. The emphasis is on what is actually learnt by each student rather than what is taught. An outcomes approach means identifying what students should achieve and focusing on ensuring that they achieve the identified outcome. Teachers focus on planning for student learning. Outcomes are written to measure the success of learning. The syllabus gives a series of outcomes agreed to be essential for all students to achieve.

Outcomes-based education

The language syllabus provides the knowledge, skills, attitudes and values that students should achieve in Grade 7. These are expressed as outcomes and indicators. These outcomes describe what the students should know, understand, value and be able to do. They are student-centred and written in terms that enable them to be demonstrated, assessed and measured.

Each learning outcome is illustrated with a list of examples called indicators. These show the kind of things that students should be able to do, know and understand to achieve an outcome. Indicators can be used by teachers to monitor student progress within a level and to make judgements about the achievement of an outcome. Learning outcomes and indicators will:

- give teachers the flexibility to develop ideas presented in the Student Book to meet the needs of their students,
- help teachers assess and report students' achievements in relation to the learning outcomes,
- allow student achievement of the outcomes to be described in consistent ways,
- help teachers monitor student learning, and
- describe what most students will know, and be able to do as a result of effective learning.

Developmental outcomes are also included. They aim to develop learners who are able to:

- reflect on and explore a variety of strategies to learn effectively,
- reflect on and explore a variety of strategies to communicate effectively,
- participate as responsible citizens in the life of local and national communities by developing their language skills, and
- be culturally sensitive across a range of social contexts.

Learning and teaching strategies

The *Language Upper Primary Teachers Guide 2003* states:

Language at upper primary is all about teaching students communication skills. To communicate effectively, students need to have a good understanding of a broad range of skills and processes. Language learning focuses on the development of the four key areas of language essential for effective communication: knowledge, skills, thinking processes, and attitudes. These are explained in the Language Upper Primary Teachers Guide 2003 *(table, page 2).*

When planning their learning and teaching strategies, teachers need to take into account this extract from the National Curriculum Statement:

By Grade 6, English is the main language of instruction across the curriculum. Vernaculars, however, must continue to be encouraged and developed. Grade 7 students must be given opportunities to express themselves in their vernacular or other national languages (Tok Pisin or Hiri Motu).

Teaching methods

The *Language Upper Primary Teachers Guide 2003* makes clear the key methods teachers should use: Language is learnt when students are actively involved in genuine activities, in a supportive environment, where the teacher responds to students' needs and interests. Vital to this are the key ideas of interactive learning, whole language, and student-centred learning.

Interactive learning

Students learn language by:

- using it to discuss ideas,
- presenting their own knowledge and expertise on a topic, and
- listening to other students present their knowledge and expertise and working creatively from each other by talking to generate, refine and extend ideas.

An example is writing a role play about an important local or national issue (Chapter 1, Student Book).

Whole language

The whole language approach is used (refer to *Language Upper Primary Teachers Guide 2003*, page 3). The skills and processes needed to help students communicate and to respond to a wide range of real and literary experiences are emphasised. Students are encouraged to respond to a wide variety of texts. The Student Book provides a wide range of genres for teachers to use and expand upon. Speaking and listening, reading and writing processes are not practised separately but as part of a whole language experience. For example, students could:

- begin with a brainstorming of a topic to be discussed,
- break into small groups to refine ideas,
- present group ideas to the class,
- write their own response to the class presentations,
- read other students' responses, and
- then discuss those responses.

Where possible, the process should be extended to the community, giving students opportunities to use language skills outside the classroom. Several activities in the Student Book show the teacher how this can be done.

In whole language, more emphasis is placed on the processes and skills than the finished product. Activities in the Student Book are broken into steps to guide students through processes of language production. Language learning takes place through communication and the integration of skills and processes.

Student-centred learning

A student-centred approach is used. It focuses on learning as being the way that students actively construct meaning, and teaching as the act of guiding and facilitating learning by:

- building on students' prior knowledge,
- using the community and its resources to provide opportunities for students to use their language skills,
- providing opportunities for problem solving, decision making and taking action, and
- providing students with opportunities to reflect upon their own learning, knowledge, values, attitudes and language skills.

The role of teachers in student-centred learning is to provide a supportive environment in which students feel confident to produce language. Teachers can use material in the Student Book to create contexts which have meaning and purpose for the students. The teacher plans and models appropriate language forms in context, and observes and supports students as they go through a process, such as that described in the example above. The teacher will intervene in the process as appropriate to provide assistance and guidance. Much of the skills development takes place in cooperative pair or group situations where students consult each other, share ideas and learn from each other.

The *Language Upper Primary Teachers Guide 2003* lists points about the role of students (page 9). Student Book activities encourage students to develop these roles.

The Guide also provides details of key skills and strategies that can be used for each of the strands (pages 10–11) and both general and specific teaching and learning strategies which are appropriate for student-centred learning (pages 14–31). These can be combined with suggestions for learning given in the Student Book, and in the following chapters of this book.

Planning guidelines

The Student Book and the Teacher Resource Book do not provide planning for term, weekly or daily lessons. You need to:

- plan groups of lessons that use models and activities in the Student Book to enable learners to achieve the outcomes described in the syllabus, and
- fit each set of lessons into a short-term work plan.

Use the table in the appendix as a checklist when planning lessons. Note that the assessing process is part of the planning process.

Assessment purpose

The purpose of assessment is to improve student learning by:

- collecting and analysing information about students' competencies,
- providing guidance, feedback and information about students' achievements and progress to students and parents, and
- helping to make decisions about improving programs and classroom organisation.

The activities in the Student Book are designed to suit these purposes.

Assessment methods

Methods chosen should answer the questions teachers ask:

- What do I want to know?
- How will I find out?

The activities provided in the Student Book help teachers assess students' abilities to demonstrate the learning outcomes. The methods used should:

- enable teachers to closely monitor and understand students' progress,
- help teachers diagnose problem areas in both learning and teaching, and
- give learners helpful feedback after every assessment.

Teachers should refer to *Language Upper Primary Teachers Guide 2003*, pages 32–49, for both general and specific guidelines for assessment. Refer to the Appendices for some useful templates.

CHAPTER 2

Speaking and listening

About this strand

Speaking and listening are together as a strand because it is usual for them to happen together. In the four chapters of this strand students will practise activities that lead to these skills:

- listening attentively to follow classroom instructions,
- listening to the teacher modelling speech,
- speaking and listening in discussions,
- speaking and listening in 'read aloud' and 'think aloud' sessions, and
- using language in different ways for different purposes, such as to persuade.

Many of the speaking and listening activities are integrated with reading and writing in both language and other subjects.

Knowledge of texts both written and oral is developed. Students learn how texts are structured in *narrative,. recount, report, procedure, explanation and exposition*. Knowledge of the written text types is used to prepare for speaking various text types and listening to various text types.

Skills that are relevant to reading and writing underpin oral skills. Students further develop the skills of *generic structure, cohesion, vocabulary, grammar, paragraphing and punctuation, word structure and procedural skills*. These are used in the specific speaking and listening skills of *interactive speaking and listening, oral presentation, grasping main points of talk, identifying particular details in talk, evaluating and reacting sensitively to what is being said, using figurative language and using and recognising non-verbal communication (gestures, facial expressions, body movements).*

Thinking processes that students will be involved in are relevant to each of the strands. They are *decision making, problem solving and strategic planning.*

Attitudes are also developed and the syllabus aims to develop students' enjoyment, confidence and independence as language users and learners. They will learn to *appreciate language, interact with others willingly with language and show that they have empathy and sensitivity towards others.*

Each chapter covers one of the outcomes. The outcomes can be used to measure students' achievements in creating and interpreting meaning from spoken language, developing spoken language and using spoken language correctly. The indicators are samples of the kind of activity you can use to check if the outcome has been reached. The indicators given in the syllabus have been used as a basis for activities in the Student Book. You can plan other activities to use as indicators of the students' achievement of the outcome.

The activities and materials in the Student Book are not divided into lessons. A teacher will decide on the outcome to be taught and then select material to achieve that outcome. Some material may be from different language strands. The templates in the Appendix will help teachers use the Student Book and this book.

Use resources in the PNG School Journals wherever possible to construct similar exercises or other exercises which help students achieve the learning outcomes.

Speaking and listening

Key words

These are words that you as a teacher, and your students, will be using in the four chapters of the Speaking and Listening strand (in order of use in the Student Book). You will find an explanation of the words in Appendix 6, the Glossary.

Student Book Chapter 1

human rights, rural, issue, discussion, persuasive, balanced, confident, gesture, expression, tone, argument, respond, situation, present, statement, commentary, open-ended, active listening, engage

Student Book Chapter 2

summarise, challenge, adapt, detailed, evidence, cause, reason, effect, result, signal, mime, clarification, refine, intonations

Student Book Chapter 3

form, purpose, audience, context, demonstration, speech map, framework, develop, chronological, organisational structures, sophisticated oral language

Student Book Chapter 4

idiom, cliché, simile, colloquial, figures of speech, figurative language, react, sympathy, empathy, sensitive

Links to other main subjects

Throughout the twelve chapters of the Student Book, the first Learning Outcome (7.1.1) *communicate a range of ideas, information and opinions about significant local and national topics to a variety of audiences* can be applied in most situations. Oral and written communication should follow this outcome. 'To a variety of audiences' emphasises the need to have close links with the community of which the school is part.

Student Book Chapter 1

Human rights, Activities 1–3: discussion on the relevance of human rights and customs in PNG society; Social Science
Health issues, Activity 4: Personal Development
Informal business, Activity 4: Making a Living
Education of girls, Activities 9–13: Personal Development, Making a Living, Maths
Our children's heritage, Activities 14–15, For you to try: conservation, sustainability; Social Science

Student Book Chapter 2

Stories of Independence, Activities 2–4: Social Science topics
Names, Activities 10–12: Social Science
Informal sector, Activities 13–16: Making a Living

Student Book Chapter 3

Stories of national emblem and national name, Activities 1–7: Social Science topics
Making an item to wear on Independence Day, Activities 8–10: creative expression, Social Science
Tsunami, For you to try: Social Science, natural hazards
Telling how to do something—Preventing malaria, Activity 11: Personal Development, Health
Cultural change, Activities 12–13: Social Science

Student Book Chapter 4

Personal Development—developing sympathy and empathy

Possible assessment tasks

Teachers should follow the assessment guides and use the templates in the *Language Upper Primary Teachers Guide 2003*, pages 32–49. On page 49, the Guide states 'Language assessment in the classroom is not about comparing one student to another. It is about assessing the skills and knowledge students have mastered and those aspects they are having difficulties with so that more focussed guidance and attention can be given to individual students.'

Some of the following activities are designed for students to measure their own achievements in terms of the outcomes for Speaking and Listening. Outcomes for Reading and Writing are also included. Students should be given chances to identify their strengths and weaknesses. The tables below will give students an opportunity to do this. Following their responses they can adjust their learning. Teachers can also use the tables as assessment guides. Any writing done should be added to the students' writing portfolios. Assessment for Speaking and Listening activities will take place mainly through observation.

You should observe and/or assess the students' ability to:

- select and talk persuasively about a range of topics,
- give or carry out instructions,
- talk with effect,
- respond to questions,
- summarise in their own understanding presented information, and
- improvise to express and interpret information modelled.

Language Upper Primary Teachers Guide 2003, page 19

Activities throughout the Student Book can be used for assessment. Students can also self-assess and be assessed by their peers. A Peer Assessment form can be found in the Guide, page 37.

Reading logs and reading journals should be kept. Any writing done should be placed in the students' writing portfolios.

Tests for Student Book Chapter 1

In Chapter 1, students learn to present information persuasively and to ask and answer questions about that information.

1. Question tags

Indicator: use pause and question tags in speaking and writing.

a) Students write the tags for the following questions.
b) Students speak the questions with the tags.

Statements	Tag answers
I can write role plays,	can't I?
You weren't listening to the question,	were you?
You know how to write questions with tags,	don't you?
You won't forget the comma next time,	will you?
I am good at speaking,	aren't I?

2. Writing and performing role plays

a) Students individually write a role play with all six question types.
b) Students identify the question types by name.
c) Students work with a partner to read the role play with correct intonation.

Ask the students to fill in this table. Students should tick items as they feel they have reached the learning outcome.

I can identify a written question from a statement.	
I can identify a spoken question from a statement.	
I know how to write different kinds of questions.	
I know how to ask questions.	
I can work with a partner to read a role play.	
I can listen to and understand other students' role plays.	

3. Writing and performing a role play discussing two sides of an issue

Indicator: *express an opinion persuasively.*
Indicator: *present two sides to an argument.*

a) Pairs of students cooperate to write a role play about an issue of their choice.
b) The role play is presented to the class.

Ask the students to fill in this table. Students should tick items as they feel they have reached the learning outcome.

I can identify an important issue.	
I can cooperate with other students to write a role play about an issue.	
I know how to write language which is persuasive.	
I can identify and write about two sides of an issue.	
I can express my point of view persuasively.	

4. A speech on an issue (in groups)

Students should use all they have learnt about expressing a point of view persuasively.

Students should write a commentary like the two in Chapter 1, Student Book.

Students should present their commentary to their group as a speech using all they have learnt about speaking persuasively.

Students should be prepared to answer questions from other students in their group.

5. Asking questions about complex issues

Indicator: *use persuasive tones and vocabulary to express a point of view and to ask focused questions.*

Students should listen to the commentaries read by other students and ask at least one focused question.

Ask the students to fill in this table. Students should tick items as they feel they have reached the learning outcome.

I can identify an issue that is important locally or nationally.	
I can decide what is my point of view about the issue.	
I can see that there are two sides to the issue and can put in some points about the opposite point of view.	
I can write a commentary about the issue using persuasive language.	
I can give a speech about an issue using my voice and body to help persuade the listener.	
I can respond to questions from my listeners.	
I can respond if my listeners have different points view.	

6. Student observation

The teacher should observe that students are able to engage with the listeners of their speech, responding to the listeners and using appropriate body language.

Tests for Student Book Chapter 2

In Chapter 2, students learn some skills and strategies for communication.

1. Cause and effect signals

Indicator: *show knowledge of signalling language used in cause and effect.*

1. Match the sentence parts in the left column with sentence parts in the right column.
2. Join the two parts together using a cause/reason or effect/result signal (some variation is possible).
3. Write the longer sentence.

1. Sir Michael Somare said we should all celebrate	9. *(this means)* they have to register a surname.
2. He said we were fortunate	5. (*in order to*) keep our culture strong.
3. He wanted to make us feel proud	2. (*as*) our Independence was a peaceful process.
4. The reporter saw people shed tears	6. (*therefore*) it is hard to tell where they come from.
5. We need to keep traditional names	10. (*because*) he was a very famous Mongolian.
6. Many people have imported names	4. (*because*) they were sad when the Australian flag was lowered.
7. Papua New Guineans were asked what their father's name was	3. (*so*) he spoke this way.
8. Mongolians need two names	1. (*because*) we had got our Independence.
9. Now that Mongolians have to have two names	8. (*because*) there are problems with record keeping.
10. Some Mongolians chose to be called Genghis Khan	7. (*as a result*) that name became a surname.

2. Ask students to fill in this table

I can identify a cause or effect signal in a sentence.	
I can tell if the signal is a cause signal.	
I can tell if the signal is an effect signal.	
I can use cause signals correctly.	
I can use effect signals correctly.	

3. Take notes on this spoken passage

Indicator: summarise main ideas from written or spoken language.

1. Teacher reads the following passage more than once.
2. Students individually write down the main points they hear.

Teacher: Read the passage slowly twice (or more if necessary). Model facial expression, gesture and intonation to communicate ideas and feelings.

The four deadliest PNG snakes

There are 106 different species of snake in Papua New Guinea. However, nearly all serious snake bites are caused by just four of them.

1. The most dangerous snake is the **Papuan taipan**. The snake is known as 'Lavai' in the Moveave District of Gulf Province and in Central Province, 'Kabagi' by the Barune people, 'Reiena Gamara' around Marshall Lagoon and 'Auguma' in Mekeo. This snake is responsible for 80% of all serious snakebites treated in Central Province. It is found in the Milne Bay, Central, Gulf and Western Provinces.

The Papuan Taipan is a very large snake. It can grow to 3.5 metres. It can move very fast. It can be very fierce if you make it angry or it feels unsafe. Sometimes the skin on top is reddish-brown. Sometimes the skin on top is almost black. Underneath can be pale or orange–red. Most have an orange stripe along the backbone.

Papuan Taipans move around during the day in the savannah grasslands and woodlands. They eat warm-blooded prey, such as rats. This means they have not been affected by eating the poisonous cane toad.

2. **The death adder** is found in all mainland Papua New Guinea Provinces. It is the most common cause of snakebites in northern Papua New Guinea. It also causes 11% of the snakebites in Central Province. Many bites happen when people step on them at night.

The snake is usually about half a metre long. But in the Markham, Ramu and Sepik valleys death adders can be one metre long. Many of these snakes have raised scales above the eyes. These look like horns. They can be many colours, for example, red, brown, grey or pale yellow. They usually have stripes of darker colour going across the body.

Death adders mostly go about at night. But during the day they hide under leaves on the ground. They use their tails to pretend to be food for lizards. When the prey comes near, the snake bites it.

3. Another snake that is found all over mainland Papua New Guinea is the **small-eyed snake**. It is not very common, however, in southern provinces. The small-eyed snake is responsible for most snakebites in the Sepik, Madang, Morobe and Oro Provinces.

The small-eyed snake can grow up to two metres long. They can be many colours. Most have a grey head, a yellowish orange neck and a pinky-grey body. There are bands of dark reddish-brown or black going across the body. Sometimes there is a lot of white and they are called 'white snake' in some areas. These snakes can be aggressive when they are disturbed. When they bite they will not let go.

The small-eyed snake mostly goes about at night. It lives in rubbish piles and is a danger to plantation workers. It eats frogs, lizards, other snakes and small mammals.

4. The **Papuan black** is usually thought to be the most dangerous snake in Papua New Guinea, but it is not. It is usually blamed for all snakebites in southern provinces and Irian Jaya, but the species is quite rare except in Western Province. Only 4% of the serious snakebites in Central Province are caused by the Papuan black. In some places this snake is now extinct.

The Papuan black snakes are usually black on the back and belly. The tip of the nose can be a lighter colour. The adult snake can be over two metres. They are thick and have large wide heads.

Frogs are the main food of the Papuan black. It is thought that they have become rare because of eating the poisonous cane toad.

Post-Courier, 'Weekend Extra', 27 August 2004, page 24

4. Take notes on this written passage

Teacher:

1. Student pairs can read the above passage in their Student Book on p. 138.
2. Provide the outline of the table.
3. They can use their notes from the oral reading and refine it and add details from reading the written passage.

The four deadliest PNG snakes

Topic	*Main idea*	*Supporting ideas*
introduction	106 snakes 4 cause most snakebites	
Papuan Taipan	dangers and location	the most dangerous in PNG 80% snakebites in the Milne Bay, Central, Gulf and Western provinces
	description	large size fast fierce colouring varies, most have an orange stripe along the backbone
	habits	day time warm-blooded prey
death adder	dangers and location	all mainland Papua New Guinea provinces source of most snakebites in northern PNG 11% of the snakebites in Central Province
	description	size 0.5 m. 'horns' of scales colouring varies, usually has darker stripes across body
		continued

Topic	Main idea	Supporting ideas
	habits	moves at night hides under leaves during day lures prey with tail
small-eyed snake	dangers and location	mostly northern provinces most snakebites in the Sepik, Madang, Morobe and Oro provinces
	description	size up to 2 m. many colours—most have grey head, darker stripes across body aggressive
	habits	goes around at night lives in rubbish piles eats frogs, lizards, other snakes and small mammals
Papuan black snake	dangers and location	southern provinces rare, so only 4% snakebites in Central Province
	description	black colour size—about 2 m. thick large, wide heads
	habits	food is frog species

5. Write a summary

Students use the table to write a summary.

6. Ask students to fill in this table

I can pick out main ideas when I hear a spoken passage.	
I can write the main ideas as notes.	
I can pick out main ideas when I read a written passage.	
I can write the main ideas as notes.	
I can fill in a table with three columns for topic, main points and supporting points.	
I can use the notes and the table to write a summary.	

7. Change the language

Indicator: *adapt language style to meet different audiences and purposes.*

Change the passage you have just read so you could tell elementary students about snakes. *Teacher:* Students can also present this as reading material for elementary students.

8. Ask students to fill in this table

I can change the language I use to suit my purpose.	
I can change the language I use to suit my audience.	

Tests for Student Book Chapter 3

In Chapter 3, students create their own examples of spoken language.

1. Speaking some instructions

Indicator: *use and sustain language and form suitable to context, purpose and audience.*

Teacher to write the instructions and recipe on the board (or copy as appropriate). Here is a recipe for taro cakes.

1. How would you talk about this recipe if you were a radio announcer.
2. Think of how you could introduce the recipe.
3. Think of what you would need to say first.
4. Remember to use the signals to show how things happen in real time. *(chronological)*
5. Finish with a concluding sentence.

Taro cakes

Ingredients:

1 taro, some ginger root, cooking oil,
1 egg, salt (small spoonful), breadcrumbs,
1 onion, tin of fish or meat, curry powder
(1 large spoonful)

Method:

Cook taro and mash.
Fry chopped onion and ginger in cooking oil.
Add meat or fish, salt, and curry powder.
Mix well and cook onion etc. together for 5 minutes.
Add the mashed taro and mix again.
Break the egg in a dish.
Put the breadcrumbs on a plate.
Cool the mixture slightly and make into small balls.
Dip each ball in the egg and then in the breadcrumbs.
Flatten the balls and fry in cooking oil until brown.

Sample answer:

Today I have a delicious recipe for you—taro cakes. You will need...Now first of all you boil...

I'm sure you will enjoy this delicious recipe.

2. Researching and giving a short speech

Students will use their *Papua New Guinea Primary School Atlas* (OUP). They should pick a topic which has enough information from either a map or a written passage.

If you have access to other source materials you may choose to have students working with them.

Students will extract information and give a speech.

They will decide on their own form, context, purpose and audience.

For example:

Students could use the map of world drought, fire and pests (*Atlas*, page 83) to show farmers that these are worldwide problems and that we need to think more about what we can do in PNG to lessen their effects. Their audience could be DAL or local farmers groups. The form could be an argument or speech with recommendations.

3. Ask students to fill in this table

I can use language to suit the context.	
I can use form to suit the context.	
I can use language to suit the purpose.	
I can use form to suit the purpose.	
I can use language to suit the audience.	
I can use form to suit the audience.	
I can identify the language structures of an oral piece.	
I can use the language structures in a speech of my own.	
I know which language structures I need to use for an argument speech and I can use them.	

Tests for Student Book Chapter 4

In Chapter 4, students become more aware of their audience and use some skills to affect their audience.

Overall Indicator: *respond sensitively in a range of formal and informal language contexts.*

Students can sympathise.	
Students can empathise.	
Students can react appropriately to other students' speeches.	
Students can recognise the absurd.	

Teachers can observe and note the responses of students as they read various passages and poems in Chapter 4.

Indicator: *effectively use a choice of language for different purposes and audiences.*

Indicator: *analyse how figurative language can deepen understanding and convey mood.*

1. Matching activity

Match the type of language suitable to the audience.

Speaking and listening

Language	*Audience*
1. Those children are as alike as two peas in a pod.	students
2. Come on, give us a go with the ball.	customers
3. You children should take turns with the ball.	friends
4. Take our golden opportunity to win a car!	business partners
5. My friends, we should listen to the Lord, and turn over a new leaf.	leader
6. I respect your point of view. However, I have a question I would like you to answer.	friends
7. Quit pulling my leg, you idiot.	playmates
8. Now it is time for us to pull together.	congregation

Answers: 1. friends, 2. playmates, 3. students, 4. customers, 5. congregation, 6. leader, 7. friends, 8. business partners.

2. Matching activity

Match the idiom or colloquialism with the meaning.

Idiom/colloquialism	*Meaning*
1. sling mud	a pest or trouble
2. take forty winks	act humbly
3. a fly in the ointment	just a small problem
4. to keep your head	behave foolishly
5. to swallow your pride	spread bad ideas
6. a storm in a teacup	behave in a sensible way
7. act the goat	to feel very happy
8. walk on air	sleep

Answers: 1. spread bad ideas, 2. sleep, 3. a pest or trouble, 4. behave in a sensible way, 5. act humbly, 6. just a small problem, 7. behave foolishly, 8. to feel very happy.

3. Written piece

Students to write a persuasive piece of four paragraphs (introduction, support, support, conclusion) using figurative language and figures of speech. They must say who their audience is. The piece should show that they understand how to use language to 'deepen understanding and convey mood'. This can be given as a speech.

4. Ask students to fill in this table

I can understand some idioms.	
I know when it is good to use idioms in my speaking and writing.	
I can understand some colloquialisms.	
I know when it is good to use colloquialisms in my speaking and writing.	
I can make my own interesting similes.	
I can use figurative language to make my writing colourful and interesting.	

Indicator: *recognise that language can have an effect on the feelings and reactions of the audience.*

Indicator: *discuss the effects different audiences can have on the speaker.*

5. Ask students to fill in this table

I recognise that it is important to know who my audience is.	
I know how to think about who my audience is.	
I know that I must choose my language to suit my audience.	
I can analyse how the language I choose can affect the feelings of my audience.	
I can choose figurative language and figures of speech that will make my audience have certain feelings.	
I understand that my audience will react to the language I use.	
I can choose figurative language and figures of speech that will make my audience react in a certain way.	

Teacher information

In this section you will find information on the activities and background to some activities in the four chapters of the Speaking and Listening strand. The information is for you to use, if you wish, in helping you plan your lessons. Any writing done during this section can be added to the students' writing portfolios.

You will find the answers to Student Book Activities in Appendix 5.

Student Book Chapter 1
Talking in different ways about things which are important

7.1.1 Communicate a range of ideas, information and opinions about significant local and national topics to a variety of audiences.

Sub-strand: Production—working out and practising the components that help us produce and use the content of our talk and writing as well as analysing how someone else has affected our emotions, interest or opinions.
The emphasis for Chapter 1 is on use—students should be given every opportunity to talk and listen to real language.

Indicators are given for some activities. However, other activities also cover these indicators. Provide extra material for students to work with wherever possible.

Activity 1: Read the role play

Indicator: use persuasive tones and vocabulary to express a point of view and to ask focused questions.

- The teacher can model reading the role play. The teacher should try to express the point of view given persuasively.
- Allow time for students to read the role play twice, exchanging characters.

Activity 2: The two sides of an issue

- Students need to understand issues in order to present their opinions. They will have plenty of opinions about things which are not issues, such as whether basketball or soccer is a better game. They could argue about this, and put forward their points of view. But a personal preference is not an issue.

Issue: An issue is an idea which is important enough to be discussed. It is an idea that people have strong thoughts about. Often people think very differently about issues. There are two or more points of view about most issues.

You can provide these boxed definitions for students to copy.

1. Revise group rules for discussion (Grade 6).
2. The issue in the role play is *letting rural people know about their human rights*. The boys' point of view is that it is good to let rural people know about their human rights, especially women.
3. The role play does not show the other side of the issue. It is called a one-sided argument.
4. Some other points of view people could have about the issue are *that things are best left as they are, without change, or that letting people know about their human rights is actually a bad thing, learning about human rights could spoil our customs.* (Your students and you may come up with other ideas.) Students need to talk confidently and persuasively about these points of view, even though they may not agree with them.

Activity 3: Write another role play with your partner

1. Make sure students are clear they are writing a different role play about the same issue.

2. Decide on your characters.
3. Write the role play from the point of view of the issue that: *things are best left as they are, without change*. Write your role play using persuasive language.
4. Students may need more modelling and practise to develop a persuasive tone of voice.
5. Students may need some modelling to help understand what is needed.

Persuasive:

When we give our point of view we try to make our listener agree with us. This is called persuasion. We make our voice sound strong and sure. We use confident* gestures and have a confident look on our face. We use persuasive words we think will make our listeners agree with us.

* confident: sure and strong

Provide some sentences for the students to practise on. For example: *I want you to try this kind of drink. It is really amazing.*

For you to try

Argument:

An argument is a discussion where you give your own point of view. The boys in the role play are giving their own thoughts or point of view. Their argument is that people need to know what their rights are so they can change customs that are bad. Other people will give a different point of view.

Students need to understand that to argue does not mean to quarrel or fight. An argument is based on persuasion, not aggression.

1. Students work in groups of four. One pair prepares the argument that human rights education will help village problems, the other pair argues that human rights education will not help village problems.
2. The two pairs get together to write a role play that argues both sides of the issue about human rights.
3. Students write their role play that has two or more characters. Encourage them to keep the characters few and simple.
4. Check that students' role plays argue both points of view evenly.
5. Check that students' characters are using persuasive language, and persuasive gestures and tone of voice.
6. The characters should listen to what other characters say. Stress again that this is not a quarrel. Students should be persuading listeners that their point of view is worth listening to.
7. Allow time for practising. If possible, also perform the role play outside the class so that students experience 'a variety of audiences'.

Listen and respond:

When students listen to a point of view, they should be thinking about how they can respond* to the ideas they are hearing. An argument does not mean that they get angry about a point of view that is different from their own. They listen, and then they respond in a persuasive way. When they write their role play, their characters should behave like this.

** respond: reply or react*

Students have learnt about conversations in Grade 6. You may need to revise the rules for turn-taking and polite conversation.

Activity 4: Another issue

➢ Teachers can use this letter to the newspaper or locate another letter more appropriate to their students' situation.

For you to try

➢ Using the letter to the editor on street selling, students write three role plays:
- play one shows a negative point of view towards street selling,
- play two shows a positive points of view towards street selling, and
- play three shows a two-sided argument that considers both points of view.

- In their role plays, students need to include examples of listening and responding as well as arguing persuasively.
- Allow time for writing and practising.
- Role plays can be performed for any available audience.

Activity 5: Important issues

- The learning outcome asks students to communicate about 'significant' local and national topics. These topics will vary from month to month, and year to year, depending on events in Papua New Guinea. Some general topics are:
  - social change
  - politics and government
  - health
  - education, or
  - the economy (including use of resources).
- *Discuss the artwork.* What is happening to the students in the cartoon? How do they feel about this?

Activity 6: Choosing an issue to talk about

Indicator: engage with the listener and respond to and use appropriate body language.

- Some suggestions are given. Teachers should think of issues that are relevant to their own students. In order to speak persuasively, students need to feel some involvement with the issue.

For you to try

Indicator: present, in a balanced speech, two sides to an argument.

- *Writing a role play*
- Students follow the steps that they have used so far, with the addition of doing research if necessary. Allow time for serious discussion and thought about the issue.
- 'Situation' means a realistic setting for the argument. For example: at a Local Government Meeting.
- You may choose to limit the issues discussed.
- *Presenting a role play*
- This role play will be shown to an audience in the school, and if possible, outside the school.
- Tell your students about answering questions after their performances, as well as asking questions after the other students' role plays. They need to be active listeners.

Activity 7: Kinds of questions

Indicator: listen carefully, and respond with understanding to questions on complex issues.

- This activity prepares students for asking questions about the role plays they will watch.
- Students read the role play (Activity 7) in groups of four. The teacher models question intonation (voice rising in tone at the end of the sentence).
- Discuss each type of question first.
- Groups should work on the table together and then present their answers to the class. Discuss the question types again as they give their answers.

Activity 8: More about question tags

Indicator: use pause and question tags in speaking and writing.

- Students will match the statement with the tag that goes with it. There are some basic rules for question tags which you can give to your students, if appropriate.
  - Point out the punctuation rule: there is a comma after the statement part of the sentence and a question mark at the end.
  - Point out that a positive statement has a negative tag and a negative statement has a positive tag.
  - Point out that some verbs have the tags do or don't, rather than a negative form of that verb:
  - *I need a ticket, don't I?*
  - *She likes the man, doesn't she?*
  - When *I am* is in the statement the tag is *aren't*: *I am going to the wedding, aren't I?*

- When they have finished, they should read the completed questions with a partner.

> Students learnt about basic question word and verb questions in Grade 6. If you feel your students need further help with these questions refer to *Improve Your Grammar Skills* in the Literacy for Papua New Guinea series, Units 24–27, by Susan Baing, Oxford University Press, 2002, and *English for Melanesia,* Book 1, Chapters 10 and 17, by Susan Baing, Oxford University Press, 1998, and *English for Melanesia,* Book 2, Chapter 6, by Susan Baing, Oxford University Press, 1999.
>
> Some of the other question types (statement type, false type) can be practised by the teacher providing examples and exercises if necessary.

- Question tags game
  1. In pairs, students prepare five questions with question tags.
  2. They write the statements (followed by a comma) on one small piece of paper and the tag (with a question mark) on another small piece of paper.
  3. Join with another pair of students.
  4. Place all ten tags and statements upside down on the desk.
  5. Take turns at turning over two pieces of paper at a time until the correct pairing of statement and tag is complete.
  6. The pair with the most correct questions wins.

Indicator: express an opinion persuasively.

Activity 9: Reading and speaking a commentary

- Students to read the article aloud in pairs.
- Allow time for reading.
- Check that students are using what they have learnt about talking persuasively.
- Vocabulary:
  - budget: the amount of money a government department has and how it decides to spend that money
  - at risk: in danger of

Activity 10: Asking questions about the commentary

- Students may need help about when they need to ask questions to find out more.
- Revise the difference between questions that are answered by yes/no and open-ended questions.
- Students should edit their own questions.

Speaking and listening

Activity 11: Finding answers to questions about important issues

Province	Total boys enrolled	Total girls enrolled	Total enrolment	Girls as a % of total	Total girls dropped out 2003–2004	% Girls dropped out of total girls enrolled	Girls re-enrolled	% Girls dropped out who re-enrolled	Girls at risk of dropping out
Western Highlands	855	717	1572	45%	191	27%	124*	65%	549 (77%)
Simbu	1458	1016	2474	41%	245	24%	270*	110%	774 (76%)
Eastern Highlands	1184	819	2003	40%	273	33%	186	68%	300 (37%)
Madang	1153	1339	2492	53%	214	16%	14	6%	637 (50%)
Morobe	1451	1164	2615	44%	183	16%	8	4%	700 (60%)
East Sepik	1155	986	2141	46%	138	14%	80	58%	633 (64%)
Total	7256	6041	13 297	45%	1202	20%	682	56%	3589 (65%)

**In two provinces,* Western *Highlands and Simbu girls returned to school when UNICEF provided equipment and materials in exchange for school fees.*

1. The table gives students information about how many girls and boys enrolled.
2. The table does not give any other information about boys.
3. This is a sample that could be applied to other provinces with reservations about how appropriate it would be for some, for example, Manus.

Activity 12: Asking questions about the commentary

➢ If you want your students to have practise at working out percentages, allow time for this. If not, provide them with the percentages as on the table above.

Activity 13: Giving answers with details

Indicator: give precise explanations in response to questions.

➢ Go over examples with students showing how information on the table can be used to give a detailed answer. Do the first question with the students to show how to get the information and express it clearly.

➢ The answers are interesting and can lead to discussion about the reasons for provincial differences.

Activity 14: Reading and speaking a commentary

➢ Allow time for reading.

➢ Students should take turns with a partner to read the commentary aloud.

➢ Check that students are using what they have learnt about talking persuasively.

➢ Vocabulary:
- heritage: what we leave for children of the future
- potential: being able to be great
- left-over scraps: little bits of nothing
- poverty line: the amount of money that you need to survive
- moral decay: doing wrong things
- gluttony: very big greediness
- prosperity: having enough of everything, such as money

➢ Your students can try to find out some answers to their questions about the heritage of our children.

➢ They might have to do some research to find out rates of population growth, or what is happening to some resources. Your Social Science work will help you.

➢ They should ask questions about the commentary, such as conservation, sustainability.

➢ They should find out some statistics about the rate we are losing forests, when various mining projects are due to close down etc.

For you to try

➢ Students can do research to see if they can find answers to the questions they have asked.

Activity 16: Questions and answers about the role play issues

➢ Make the written role plays available in class so students can refer to them when writing questions.

Student Book Chapter 2
Some skills for talking to other people

7.1.2 Use a wide range of presentation skills and strategies to communicate effectively in informal and formal school contexts and the wider community.

Sub-strand: Skills and strategies—acknowledging the importance of skills and strategies necessary to effectively communicate.

Indicators are given for some activities. However, other activities also cover these indicators. Provide extra material for students to work with wherever possible.

Some words that will probably be new to your students are used in the articles in Chapter 2. These should be dealt with in context.

Activity 1: Re-telling a familiar story

- This is an introductory activity. Define familiar. All students in the group should know the same story.

Activity 2: Reading familiar stories

Indicator: refine facial expression, gesture and intonation for communicating ideas and feelings.

- Check that students are using all they have learnt about facial expression, using the body and tone of voice.

Activity 3: Talking about the two passages

- Students should be able to recognise that different styles of language are being used.

Activity 4: Adapting language

Indicator: adapt language style to meet different audiences and purposes.

- Make sure that students change the language rather than the message.

Activity 5: Asking questions about a familiar story

Indicator: use questions to seek clarification about familiar stories, events or people.

- Discuss the role of questions in the role play.
- Revise question types if necessary.

Activity 6: Talking about the questions

- Use the question classification given in Chapter 1.

For you to try

- Use questions to get more information.
- Research a story, event or person
- Go through the instructions with the students. After classroom preparation, they will need to do this outside school hours.
- Students can choose a story, an event or person. Or teachers may want them to do more than one topic. A repeat of the research and preparation process could be done as assessment.

Activity 7: Reporting on your questions

- This is a feedback exercise with oral reporting of results of questioning.
- Students should be able to analyse the results of their questioning and to look at their own behaviour and methods during the interviewing.

Activity 8: Writing a longer story, account of an event or description of a person

- The accounts written after expansion from the questioning can be illustrated and left in the classroom for other students to read.
- This activity forms the basis for the next activity in which students transform writing at Grade 7 level into simpler form.
- These stories can be illustrated and left for elementary students to read for themselves.

Activity 9: A new audience and purpose

Indicator: adapt language style to meet different audiences and purposes.

- Students at Grade 3 level are still studying in other languages in the classroom. Tell your students to make allowance for this.

Activity 10: Talk about names

- This is an introductory activity.
- Use examples from your own vernacular. There are books about the origin of English names (both first names and surnames). Here are a few examples:
- *English surnames*

- Smith—this comes from the now gone activity of the Smithy—a business which worked iron metal into various items, especially shoes for horses.
- Fitz(Gerald), Mac(Robert) and (Robert)son—all show descent from a particular named person.
- *English first names*
- Susan—the lily
- Leo—like a lion
- Rex—the king
- *Some vernacular names*
- Naisgai—to chop wood
- Uruts—man of the sea.

Activity 11: Read this article to a partner

- Check that students are using all they have learnt about facial expression, using the body and tone of voice.

Activity 12: Talking about the article on names

Indicator: *challenge a point of view with supporting evidence.*

- Students can work in pairs to read the speech and to interrupt and challenge ideas in the speech as appropriate.
- They should use polite language, for example, 'That is an interesting idea, but I don't agree. Instead…' and provide evidence to support their challenge.

For you to try

- Students will first prepare a speech putting forward their own ideas about names and read this speech to a partner. The partner challenges as above.

Activity 13: Read this article to a partner

- Check that students are using all they have learnt about facial expression, using the body and tone of voice.

Activity 14: Cause and effect

Indicator: *show knowledge of signalling language used in cause and effect.*

- Teachers should start by giving several examples of cause/reason and effect/result sentences and talking about some of the words that are used as signals to show this relationship of ideas in a sentence.
- Students then read the article again to note where the signals are used and what kind of relationship they show.
- Draw up the table on the blackboard to fill in after students have completed their own tables.
- Discuss each sentence showing how the signal word or phrase helps the listener understand the relationship of ideas in sentences.

Activity 15: Making a summary

Indicator: *summarise main ideas from written or spoken language.*

- Students work in pairs to find main points.

Activity 16: Using information

- Use the information in the commentary to prepare a short report to be read to your Local Government Council.
- Use a pyramid structure for the discussion—begin with pairs, then four, then the whole class.
- If possible, some reports should be presented in a realistic situation.

Activity 17: Using cause and effect signals

- Students work in pairs to decide on the signals to be used at the marked places.
- They then individually re-write the passage to include the signals.
- The re-written passage can be read to another pair and discussion should take place about each of the signals used.

Activity 18: Have some fun

Indicator: refine facial expression, gesture (and intonation) for communicating ideas and feelings.

1. Talk about gestures and explore differences. You may need to demonstrate some expressions and gestures.
2. Students can choose their own topic with approval from the teacher.
3. Allow time for preparation.

➢ The role plays can be put on as a performance outside the classroom.

Student Book Chapter 3
Using different ways of talking and listening

7.1.3 Create own examples of spoken language demonstrating various ways it can be adapted to suit different but familiar contexts.

Sub-strand: Contexts and texts refer to the importance of learning and using language in different situations and the fact that how we communicate influences the kind of text we use. Indicators are given for some activities. However, other activities also cover these indicators. Provide extra material for students to work with wherever possible.

Indicator: use and sustain language and form suitable to context, purpose and audience.

Activity 1: Our National Emblem

➢ This activity is a preparation stage for the following activities.

➢ The finding meaning activity must focus on meaning in context, as the word is used in the passage.

Activity 2: Explaining our National Emblem 1 and 2

➢ In pairs, students should spend time to adapt the language in the passage so it can be understood by themselves and by younger students.

➢ You will need to provide copies of the National Emblem for the younger students to use. (See Figure 2.1.)

➢ Your students will know if their explanations have been understood by their audience if the younger students are able to colour the emblem correctly, or label the colour of the part.

➢ If you cannot copy the emblem, ask your students to draw their own copy from the Student Book on p. 27.

Activity 4: The national name of Papua New Guinea

- Students follow the steps for Activity 1.

Activities 5 and 6: Explaining our national name 1 and 2

- Students follow the steps for Activities 2 and 3.
- Work in a group of three or four.
- Your students will need to prepare the 'game' before the visit to the classroom of the younger children.
  1. Each group of students prepares twelve cards.
  2. Six of the cards will be dates, the other six will be names. (Copy and cut the cards template into 12 pieces.)

1520	**Papua**
1545	**New Guinea**
Dutch, German and English 1884	**New Guinea**
Australia 1906	**Papua**
Australia 1949	**Territory of Papua and New Guinea**
Ist July 1971	**Papua New Guinea**

Cards template for the game

  3. After presenting the information to the younger students, your students will tell them the rules of the game.
  4. If at first the younger students do not succeed in matching the cards, your students may need to present the information again.
  5. The game can be a straight matching game with all the cards exposed right side up and the younger students taking turns to match them, or it can be played as a memory game—students take turns to turn over two cards. If they think they match they can claim the cards, but the other students can challenge this. If the cards do not match or they are successfully challenged (wrong) turn the cards wrong side up again and the next student tries. Continue until all cards are matched. The student with the most pairs wins.
- The students can practise the game themselves.

Activity 7: Explaining our national name 3

1. The teacher will need to find suitable places for the students to perform, for example, the church grounds, market, Local Level Government (LLG) offices, health clinic.
2. Students will need to work out what each character should say, and the language they should use to say it.
3. The students will be in groups of six. There are twelve roles. The students will take two roles each.
4. They will need to work out a sequence so that the first six roles are played, followed by the second six roles in order. For example:

student 1	historical Indonesian
student 2	Portuguese
student 3	Ynigo Otriz de Retes of Spain
student 4	Dutch German and English
student 5	Australian 1906
student 6	Australian 1949
student 1	Editor of *South Pacific Post*
student 2	reader of possible names
student 3	Ade Ole Anna Asisa
student 4	Paulus Arek
student 5	Papuans
student 6	Percy Chatterton

Activity 8: Explaining how to do something

1. Students number steps 1 to 9. They need to think about what should be done first in real time.
2. The steps should be written as instructions.
3. Revise use of verbs, such as collect, tie, sew.

Activity 9: Talking about making a wig

➢ Students can write out a speech with signals and read it.

For you to try

➢ *Explaining how to do something*

➢ Students will need time to research and find out the method of making a traditional item to wear or use on Independence Day.

Activity 10: Role play—'Visitors to the school'

➢ Check that the language used is appropriate to the context, purpose and audience.

➢ Allow time for practising and performance.

For you to try

Yar—casuarina (*Casuarina equisetifolia*)

kalapulin/kalopilum—calophyllum (*Calophyllum inophyllum*)

mound—a lightly higher piece of ground

➢ The teacher will need to identify the audience for the students as appropriate. The students who can then suit their speech to the audience.

➢ Allow time for research and planning.

➢ Students may want to illustrate their speech.

Activity 11: Telling how to do something: Preventing malaria

1. This activity and the practical talk that follows are done as group work.
2. The teacher will need to identify the audience for the students as appropriate. The audience is told to the students who can then suit their speech to the audience. A good audience would be mothers at the health clinic or sellers and buyers at the market.

For you to try

➢ Students in groups should present their talk in a real situation. Although they will not have the tablet they can show how to immerse a net in a bucket of water and hang it to dry in the shade.

Activity 12: Presenting a point of view

Indicator: show knowledge of more sophisticated language structures as in an argument.

➢ Teacher to put outline of speech map on board for students to copy.

➢ Teacher to read the following speech.

Activity 13: Make a summary of a point of view

➢ Students should use the speech map and list the following:

➢ Title

➢ Introduction:
- topic
- issue
- point of view

➢ 1st support

➢ 2nd support

➢ conclusion

➢ recommendation

For you to try

Indicator: use correct organisational structures for sophisticated oral language.

1. Allow time for research and planning.
2. Students must practise before they present their speeches.

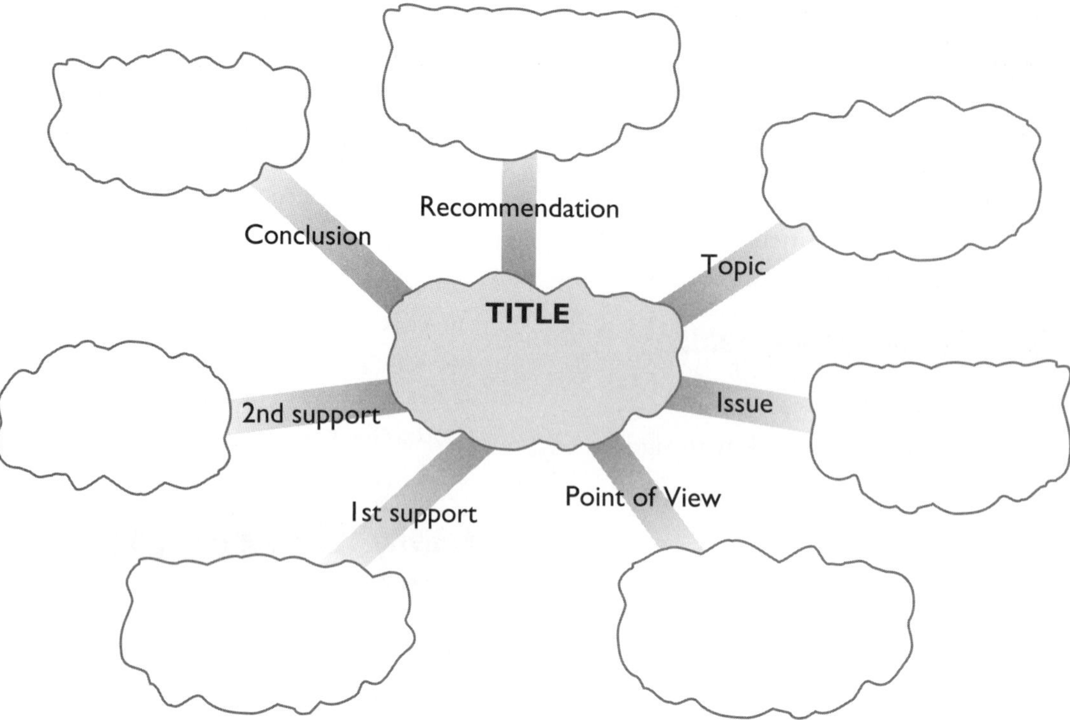

Our culture must change (based on the editor's opinion, *The National*, 19 September 2003, page 18)	Title
This year we saw two different faces of PNG culture on display. Firstly, there was the Goroka Show. This is an amazing show that displays the tribal culture of the country to the world. At the same time, at the Yacht Club in Port Moresby, there was an art exhibition of art that is being done in PNG today. There is a belief in PNG that 'culture' means only 'traditional culture'. However, this is not true. Can the culture of a country stay the same for ever? Traditional culture is of course a very important part of our culture, but there is a modern culture as well. It is important that we see the two parts to our culture side by side. It is very important to preserve PNG's traditional culture, but it is also very important to have a modern culture.	topic issue point of view
Firstly, just how traditional is the culture we see at shows? We see dances that have been changed. We see trade store paints being used to paint faces and bodies. But does this mean our ancestors would not have used such things if they could buy them? In the past the Goroka Show was a time of great excitement, a giant celebration of beauty, strength and the certainty of tradition. But shows like the Goroka Show are changing. And they must change. It is false to expect the show to be the same year after year. In the end the culture we are trying to preserve will not survive.	1st support
The display of the art of today showed how wonderful modern painting, sculpture and other art forms are. But this kind of culture does not get the same support as traditional culture. This makes me think that people do not understand the role played by culture of our parents and grandparents. Modern art is a way of celebrating and preserving those traditions. It is also a way of showing how traditions are changing and what life is like today. Our descendants can view this art and know what our culture was like.	2nd support
It is clear that we need to preserve our traditional culture. But at the same time we must help those artists of today to develop our culture of today. A lot of education, time and money has been spent on our past. Now we must do the same for our present and future.	conclusion
The people and government of PNG have to see that both traditional and modern art go side by side and support our modern artists in the same way.	recommendation

3. The teacher should ask each student what their context, purpose and audience are while they are in the planning stage.
4. You can use this activity to assess the students' attainment of the learning outcome.

Student Book Chapter 4
Thinking critically about your own speaking and listening

7.1.4 Assess the relevance, appropriateness and quality of their own speaking and listening in relation to the purpose and audience.

Sub-strand: Critical literacy: selecting and evaluating information researched, leading to making informed choices and opinions.

Indicators are given for some activities. However, other activities also cover these indicators. Provide extra material for students to work with wherever possible.

Overall Indicator: respond sensitively in a range of formal and informal contexts.

Indicator: effectively use a choice of languages for different purposes and audiences, such as idioms, similes, colloquialisms and persuasive argumentative language.

Activity 1: What is an 'idiom'?

1. Students to read the poem. They should realise that each line is an idiom.
2. Work in groups of six. There are eight idioms. Do two to show the students how to approach the activity.
3. Demonstrate how to fold the paper.
4. Do not expect students to reach the right answer with each idiom. Some are clearer than others.

Activity 2: Using idioms

➢ Students will probably try to model their work on the poem in Activity 1. Do *not* try to restrict their use of idioms. The piece can be a poem, letter or description.

Activity 3: Using idioms properly

➢ Students can re-write their piece from Activity 2 or write a new piece to be read. This time they should use a few effective idioms.

Activity 4: Writing and speaking again

1. The poem in Activity 1 can be written in formal terms and then read aloud. No idioms should be used.
2. Students can decide on the situation and audience and choose the appropriate language.

Activity 5: What are similes?

➢ Similes are sometimes over-used. Some of those listed have lost their effectiveness and become stale.

Activities 6 and 7: Using similes properly

➢ Students should see the difference between the fresh similes used in the passage and the common ones in the table.

Activity 8: Colloquial language

➢ Students read the sentences aloud and note the differences.

Activity 9: Match the meanings

➢ As with idioms and similes, common colloquialisms can grow stale with overuse.

Activities 10 and 11: Colloquial language needs to be used carefully

➢ The conversation makes no sense because it is mostly a series of idioms and colloquialisms. Students should see that this is not an effective use of these figures of speech.

For you to try 1 and 2

1. Students have practise in the appropriate use of colloquialisms.

2. The dialogue is then written without colloquialisms.

Indicator: analyse how figurative language can deepen understanding and convey mood in a play or speech.

Activities 12 and 13: Figurative language

- Students should see the use of figurative language. They should not be afraid of Shakespeare because this is English, though the English of his time.

Activities 14 and 15: Using word pictures

- The cloze exercise shows that poets choose their language very carefully to create the picture they want.

Indicator: recognise that language can have an effect on the feelings and reactions of the audience.

Indicator: discuss the effects different audiences can have on a speaker.

Activities 16 and 17: The use of figurative language in a passage

- The writer uses figurative language in a way that is not over-done. This is the way good writers use figurative language.

Activity 18: How the choice of language affects the audience

- W. Somerset Maugham published this story in a collection called *On a Chinese Screen* in 1922. The feelings that he had at the time are still relevant today.
- He begins by making us feel secure with a pleasing description; then suddenly we see that this is not a pretty picture of rural happiness, but a social comment.
- The students should realise that this is a deliberate choice by the writer. He has chosen his words for this purpose. He wants to shock his listener into thinking about the issue of human rights.
- Students should show that they sympathise (feel sorry for) and empathise with (can understand the feelings of) the coolies.
- *Coolie*—a day labourer, the means of transport for market goods, road making materials etc.
- *Candle extinguisher*—a cone shape, with a broad brim

Activity 19: Who is your audience?

- Students have talked about audiences before. This activity helps them focus their ideas. Stress that they are not writing and speaking for themselves, but for an audience.

For you to try

- This activity could be done by poetry writing, letter writing, speech writing or article writing. Allow students to choose which genre they want to write in. They should think about their audience (and should tell the class who their imaginary audience is before reading their piece).

Chapter 3 Reading

About this strand

When teaching reading skills, teachers need to keep in mind the language principles stated in the *Language Upper Primary Teachers Guide 2003.*

In the four chapters of this strand, students will practise activities that lead to these understandings:

- that reading is for enjoyment, for locating information and for making meaning,
- that good readers know what processes they use when they are reading,
- that good readers know how to make predictions. They base this on what they know about words, about the correct use of words and correct sentences, how certain kinds of writing are structured, and what they know about the topic before they start reading,
- that good readers know that there are several skills they can use to help them find and remember the meaning of what they are reading, and
- that good readers think about what they have read. They make judgements about what they have read. They base these judgements on their own values and on their own experiences of the world.

based on *Language Upper Primary Teachers Guide 2003,* page 6

The areas of knowledge, skills, thinking and attitudes are developed in the Student Book:

1. Students' knowledge of written texts is developed. Students learn through reading how texts are structured in *narrative, recount, report, procedure, explanation, exposition, and graphic representation.*
2. Various skills are learnt to develop students' competencies in learning and using language in a broad range of contexts: *generic structure, cohesion, vocabulary, grammar, paragraphing and punctuation, word structure and procedural skills.*
3. Thinking processes are those in which students' inner ideas, feelings and images are accessed, rearranged and presented. The processes of *decision making, problem solving and strategic planning* are used in reading.

Attitudes are also developed and the syllabus aims to develop students' enjoyment, confidence and independence as language users and learners. They will learn to *appreciate language, interact with others willingly with language and show that they have empathy and sensitivity towards others.*

Each chapter covers one of the outcomes. The outcomes can be used to measure students' achievements in creating and interpreting meaning from written language. The indicators are samples of the kind of activity you can plan to allow you to see if the outcome has been reached. The indicators given in the syllabus have been used as a basis for activities in the Student Book. Many of the reading activities in the Student Book are integrated with speaking and listening and writing in both Language and other subjects. You can plan other activities that can be used as indicators of the students' achievement of the outcome.

The activities and materials in the Student Book are not divided into lessons. A teacher will decide on the outcome to be taught and then select material for that outcome. Some material may be from different Language strands. The templates in the Appendix will help teachers use the Student Book and this book.

Use resources in the PNG *School Journals* wherever possible to construct similar exercises or other exercises which help students achieve the learning outcomes.

Key words

These are words that you as a teacher, and your students, will be using in the four chapters of the Reading strand (in order of use in the Student Book). You will find an explanation of the words in Appendix 6, the Glossary.

Student Book Chapter 5
orientation, build-up, complications, pace, resolution, statistics, factual texts, literary text, fairy story, preference, action, dialogue, description, diagram, table

Student Book Chapter 6
style, impersonal style, personal style, scan, scanning, skim, skimming, acknowledge, sources

Student Book Chapter 7
influence, narrator, narrative, first person, third person, cultural identity, attitudes, image

Student Book Chapter 8
match, contractions, critically, generalisation, personal, emotive language, repetition, effective

Links to other main subjects

Student Book Chapter 5
Family life, role of women, Activities 5 and 7: Personal Development
Caring for a child with malaria, Activity 15: Health

Student Book Chapter 6
The Neem Tree, Making a living, Agriculture
LLGs, Social Science
When Pig met Potato!, Social Science
Mt Sion Centre for the Blind, Personal Development

Student Book Chapter 7
Cultural identity, Social Science

Student Book Chapter 8
Death Penalty, Personal Development
Development of forest resources, Social Science

Possible assessment tasks

The following activities are designed for students to measure their own achievements in terms of the Outcomes for Reading. Outcomes for Speaking and Listening and Writing are also included.

Teachers should follow the assessment guides and use the templates in the *Language Upper Primary Teachers Guide 2003*, pages 32–49.

Some of the following activities are designed for students to measure their own achievements in terms of the outcomes for Reading. Teachers can also use these tables as assessment guides. Activities throughout the Student Book can be used for assessment.

Assessment for Reading activities will take place mainly through observation of students at work—their reading behaviours and strategies used.

Observations take place before, during and after reading. Assessment takes place during:

- silent reading
- small group interaction
- shared reading, and
- discussion.

Students can also be assessed through their written responses. Reading logs and reading journals should be kept. Any writing done should be placed in the students' writing portfolios.

Tests for Student Book Chapter 5

In Chapter 5, students learnt to look closely at a wide range of more complex texts.

1. Ideas and information in a text

Provide a story for students to read and answer questions. Base your questions on *Language Upper Primary Teachers Guide 2003*, page 25. Use a story from the *Senior School Journal* or one of your other class sets.

2. Students to analyse how the story starts and to draw a plan of the story.

3. Ask students to fill in this table

I can find information in a text.	
I can find ideas in a text.	
I can understand the author's point of view in a text	
I can try to work out new vocabulary in a text.	
I can analyse how a story starts.	
I can see how a story begins, builds up, has complications and resolution.	
I can see how different stories do this in different ways.	
I can see that different stories move at a different pace.	

4. Graphs and pictures in texts

a) How does this table help people to understand some facts about tsunamis?

History's great tsunamis

1755	Portugal, Spain, Morocco	60 000 dead
1883	Krakatoa volcanic eruption	36 000 dead
1896	Japan	27 000 dead
1906	Columbia	1500 dead
1946	Aleutian Island and Alaska after earthquake	105 dead
1975	Hawaii after earthquake	2 dead
1992	Nicaragua	30 dead
1994	Mindoro	41 dead
1994	East Java	200 dead
1996	Peru	12 dead
1998	Papua New Guinea	2200 dead
2004	Indian Ocean	about 300 000

Students should say that tsunamis are capable of killing many people; that they can come from earthquakes or volcanic eruptions; that they have happened many times in history.

b) Use 'Fishing Nets for Flying Foxes', *School Journal Senior,* 2, 2002, or 'Hundreds and

Reading

Hundreds of Rectangles', Senior, 2, 2003. How do the pictures help you understand the text?

5. Ask students to fill in this table

I can understand how diagrams and pictures support a text.	
I can understand that a table makes statistics clear in a text.	
I can see that diagrams and tables add to the readers' understanding of text.	
I can see that there are many ways to treat facts in text.	
I understand that some ways suit some audiences and other ways suit other audiences.	

Tests for Student Book Chapter 6

Teachers can use a suitable passage for these assessments. The passage should be in impersonal style and contain facts. If teachers use the passage on art below, their students will be able to read it in their Student Book on p. 139.

1. Scanning

What kind of information would you look for to find an answer by scanning?

Students should be able to give detailed things they would look for.

Which provinces are famous for their baskets? Look for province name and find the word basket near it.

Where would you find gope? Look for the word gope and a place name near it.

When did traditional art start to get taken away from PNG? Look for a date and words, such as taken away.

Who are some famous modern artists? Look for names under a heading or topic sentence that has the words modern art in it.

What sort of useful objects are decorated by village craftsmen? Look for key words useful, decorated, village craftsmen.

Now scan and find the answers.

2. Skimming

Skim the article below to find the main points.

Art

Traditional art ranges from objects used for everyday activities, such as hunting or betelnut chewing, to those used for religious purposes. The designs are the same as they were in traditional times. This is because they have special meaning in the community.

The Papuan Gulf regions and Sepik–Ramu regions are particularly noted for their traditional art. In the Gulf area, art objects are mostly flat, such as *gope* (ancestral boards) or bull-roarers. The Sepik–Ramu art is more three-dimensional. Objects are masks, house-hooks, and building decorations. The *malanggan* carvings of New Ireland are famous. These are very detailed carvings used for ceremonies. They combine snake, bird, fish and human images. Baskets from Milne Bay and Bougainville, pottery from Central, Morobe and Madang, and bilums from the Sepik and Highlands are also special art forms.

Since European contact in the late 1880s, many fine examples of PNG traditional art have been taken out of the country. These objects are kept in museums in Australia, Germany, the United Kingdom and the United States of America. Some of these objects have been sent back to our own museum. One of the main roles of the National Museum and Art Gallery is to stop the destruction or illegal export of important traditional art.

Today many village craftsmen produce 'tourist art'. These are objects made for sale to visitors. They can be simple carvings or painted gourds from the Trobriands to animal forms from Milne Bay or Bougainville.

A 'modern art' has developed through teaching at schools and university. Many people now make a living selling art on canvas or paper at craft markets. The style of the art still owes a lot to traditional art, but often the materials used are modern. Some modern artists, such as Kauage and Akis have become famous here and overseas.

3. Identify the features of factual texts

Read the text in full and comment on the impersonal style.

4. Look for detailed information in reading

Ask students to write answers with details after you read the text in full.

1. Does PNG have a strong tradition in art? Yes.
2. Did traditional art change much? No. What was the reason? Because they had special meaning in the community.
3. What were the two main uses of art in traditional times? To decorate everyday objects and for religious and ceremonial purposes.
4. Does art only mean carved or painted objects? No—it includes baskets, pots and bilums.
5. What objects are part of your own traditional art?
6. Where are a lot of the traditional art objects of PNG? In overseas museums.
7. Do you think traditional art should be allowed to be kept outside PNG?
8. What is the work of PNG's museum? To stop destruction and export of traditional art.
9. Do you think art should be taught in schools?
10. Do you think traditional designs should be used in tourist art?

5. Use questions to help you find out more information

Students should be given the opportunity to form questions that will help them find out more about traditional and other art and if possible to do research to find answers.

6. Ask students to fill in this table

I can ask myself questions that will help me think about what I already know about a topic.	
I can ask myself questions to help me get information from a piece of writing.	
I can scan to find answers to questions in a passage.	
I can skim to find main ideas in a passage.	
I can find detailed answers to information in a piece of writing.	
I can think about ideas that come from that piece of writing and give my own point of view.	
I know where to go to get more answers.	
I can recognise impersonal style and understand how to use it in writing.	
If I use ideas or facts from a book or article I know that I must say where they came from.	

Tests for Student Book Chapter 7

1. How students feel about a narrative

Choose a story that students will react to from the *PNG School Journal* or class set, such as *Island Life*.

Ask them to write a personal response to the story.

Ask them to identify how the author has made them feel that way.

Some suggestions:

Island Life by Kumalau Tawali: 'From the other world', 'A wash in coconut water', 'Breaking the ear'

Climbing Mountains by Daniel Kumbon, Chapter 3 'Hardships ahead'

Fact or Fiction by Joe Kanekane

2. Why authors choose their story endings

Use the available stories to get students to analyse the ending of a story.

3. The narrator

Students should identify the narrator in a story, say whether the narrator is first or third person, analyse how this affects the story and say how the author's choice influences how the reader feels.

4. Ask students to fill in this table

I am able to respond to a story.	
I can see how a writer uses their writing skill to make me feel a certain way about a story.	
I can analyse the way a writer ends a story.	
I can identify the narrator of a story and see why the writer used that kind of narrator.	

5. Cultural identity in stories

Use available stories to get students to write a response to the way cultural identity is treated in a story.

How does the attitude of the writer, the beliefs of the writer and the social customs of the writer affect how they write the story, and how the student feels about the story.

6. Ask students to fill in this table

I understand that cultural identity is an important theme in stories from different nations.	
I can analyse a cultural identity theme and see that there are both similarities and differences to my own culture.	
I can recognise that the cultural identity of a writer can have an affect on how I understand and respond to a story.	
I can recognise that the knowledge of a writer can have an affect on how I understand and respond to a story.	
I can recognise that the experiences of a writer can have an affect on how I understand and respond to a story.	

Tests for Student Book Chapter 8

1. Purpose and audience

The learning outcome states that students will learn to assess the relevance, appropriateness and quality of texts in relation to purpose and audience.

Use a variety of texts for assessment, such as instructions, stories, articles. You can find these in the *PNG School Journal* and other sources.

Students can fill in worksheets for a number of texts. They should consider all they have learnt about audience and purpose.

Title:

Type of text (letter, instructions, opinion etc.):

Type of language (formal/informal):

Audience:

Purpose:

Relevance of text to audience and purpose:

Appropriateness of text to audience and purpose:

Quality of text appropriate for audience and purpose:

2. Ask students to fill in this table

I know that style, word choice, sentence structure, punctuation and tone all reflect the writer's idea of the audience and purpose they are writing for.	
I can recognise formal and informal language.	
I know that formal language and informal language each have areas where they are the appropriate kind of language.	
I know that language must be matched to audience and purpose, for example, technical language.	
I know that the text must be relevant to the purpose.	

3. Critical appraisal of issues

Teachers can make copies of the report below or use another report about a current issue.

Read this report and comment critically on it.

'Guns' popular child toy

A Madang primary school has confiscated 400 toy pistols from its students. The school wants to crackdown on the carrying of these toys to school. Parents and guardians have signed a petition to the Governor calling for the banning of toy guns being sold in shops.

The guns were taken from the students and given to police.

The students began to bring the guns after one of their former school students was shot by police during an armed hold-up. They were using the toys for life-like games around the school.

The Chairman of the guns control committee said that this was the first school in PNG to take such a step. He said the teachers were a shining example. He said that it was very important the children be taught to reject toy guns and war-like games.

Post-Courier, 3 May 2005, page 2

Reading

Students should comment on

- 'guns' in headline,
- use of a number 400,
- reasons for this large number given,
- action taken, and
- idea in final sentence.

4. Ask students to fill in this table

I can recognise the difference between fact and opinion.	
I can see that people sometimes write opinion as if it is fact.	
I can see that people can use bias when they express opinion, and in the way they choose their facts.	
I can recognise emotive language.	
I can recognise a generalisation.	
I can understand what makes a piece of writing about an issue effective.	
I can see that there are two sides to issues and can justify my support of one side.	

Teacher information

In this section you will find information on the activities, and background to some activities in the four chapters of the Reading strand. The information is for you to use, if you wish, in helping you plan your lessons.

There are some key skills and processes that teachers need to use for teaching reading using the Student Book. These key skills and processes apply to any reading task you give your students.

Reading effectively means using a three-stage process. Each time a reading task is approached, decide how you can best use these three stages:

1. Before reading students should:
   - look,
   - talk,
   - share their ideas in a pair or group situation, and
   - make predictions about any text and any diagrams, graphs or pictures that accompany the text.
2. During reading students should:
   - join in the reading,
   - read on further in the text or read back in the text,
   - use pictures or graphs that accompany the text to help them interpret the text,
   - make mental pictures of their own,
   - attempt to clarify what they are reading,
   - make use of cues from the meaning of words, the sounds of letters and letter groups and grammatical structures of sentences, and
   - attempt to sound out and discover the meaning of unknown words.
3. After reading students should:
   - talk about what they have read,
   - think about the content, ideas and issues in what they have read,
   - share their thoughts with other students in a pair or group situation,
   - compare their own thoughts with other students and justify their ideas,
   - practise substituting words or ideas or writing new endings to stories,
   - go beyond the text they have read and make comments, and
   - analyse the content.

The *Language Upper Primary Teachers Guide 2003*, pages 19–27, provides reading strategies for the teacher to use in teaching reading. These can be applied to the activities in the Student Book.

You will find the answers to Student Book Activities in Appendix 5.

Student Book Chapter 5 Reading and Responding

7.2.1 Read and respond to a wide range of more complex literary and factual texts.

Sub-strand: Production—working out and practising the components that help us produce and use the content of our talk and writing as well as analysing how someone else has affected our emotions, interest or opinions.

Overall Indicator: interpret information and ideas in texts through close study.

Indicator: compare and discuss differences in build-up, complications, pace and resolutions in different stories.

Activities 1–8 Reading stories and answering questions in a close study of the text.

1. Reading can be done aloud in pairs.
2. The questions can be answered in pairs and then those answers compared with those of another pair.
3. New vocabulary can be attempted in context and recorded in a vocabulary book.

Activity 1: Read this story

- Begin with a telling or reading of the fairy story 'Jack and the Beanstalk'.

Activity 3: Read this story

- Begin with a discussion about practical jokes—are they a good thing? Have you ever done one or been on the receiving end of one? Do you know about any really funny ones that have happened?

Activity 5: Read this story

- Discuss any family stories you have where something funny happened.

Activity 7: Read this story

- How much help does your mother get from you and your family? Do you think she would like you to help more? What could she do about it?

Indicator: discuss and give examples of why the work of some authors is especially enjoyed by teenage boys and girls.

Activity 9: Your ideas about the stories you have read

- Some stories are more popular with teenagers than others.
- This could be that they appeal to a sense of humour; they show the reality of the teenage world; and so on.

Activity 10: Story plans

- Students should work in groups and discuss each story before they attempt to map it. They may not be able to fit the stories to the plan. This is not a problem and they should make it clear in their discussion that that story is different.

Indicator: read and analyse the impact on the reader of different ways of starting a story, for example, dialogue, action, description.

Activity 11: How stories start

- Stories can begin in many ways, for example, with action, dialogue or description.

Activity 12: Analysing how stories start

- An effective start to a story draws the reader in. We often glance at the first sentences of a book to decide if we want to read it. Some first lines are very famous. For example from *Anna Karenina* by Leo Tolstoy 'All happy families resemble one another; every unhappy family is unhappy in its own way.'
- Students should add any books or other stories (for example, those in the *School Journal*) to their record.

- Refer students to class sets, for example, *Island of the Blue Dolphins*.

Indicator: convey how graphs or statistics can support an argument or improve understanding of information in factual texts.

Activities 13 and 14: Diagrams and tables in factual texts

- Sometimes stories we read have pictures (illustrations) or maps and diagrams to help us understand the story. Factual texts have ways other than written text to add to our information and help us understand.
- Make use of any texts you have with diagrams or tables. Your Oxford PNG *Atlas* has many statistics that can be used.
- Newspaper articles sometimes contain up-to-date data.

Indicator: contrast literary and factual treatments of a locally relevant health issue.

- Malaria has been used as an example. You can provide other texts that are about locally relevant health issues. There are 'comic books' on AIDS and related issues available from Helt Promosen, PO Box 807, Waigani.

Activity 15: Some different ways of presenting facts

- If malaria is relevant to you, begin by asking what your students usually do if they think they have malaria. If you are using another health issue, provide the students with facts. They can then write their own literary texts.

Activity 16: Talking about different ways to present facts

For you to try

- Students can be asked to write a play to present to mothers at the market.

Student Book Chapter 6
Reading for knowledge

7.2.2 Apply a range of strategies to locate relevant information and make meaning of literary and factual texts.

Sub-strand: Skills and strategies—acknowledging the importance of skills and strategies necessary to effectively communicate.

Overall Indicator: read a range of explanatory texts, investigating and noting impersonal style.

Indicator: propose initiatives in seeking references and sources of information.

Activity 1: Why do we read?

- Resources in schools will be limited, so do not neglect your local experts.

Activity 2: Factual texts

- In pairs, read about neem trees.

Activity 3: The main points

- Filling in the table prepares students for considering impersonal style.

Activity 4: The style of factual articles

- Impersonal or objective writing puts a distance between the writer and the reader. The article on neem trees is objective writing. The other articles are also objective, but to a lesser degree.
- The passive voice is used when the doer of the action is not known, or when the doer of the action is less important than the action. Active verbs involve the doer and are more personal. Passive verbs are more impersonal. Some sentences can be changed from one to the other, such as the example on the table below. Others need to have a subject added if they are changed into the active: *The rat could be heard in the roof.* → *They heard the rat in the roof.*
- If students are unsure about passive tense they can do this exercise:

Passive	*Active*
Disease is carried by flies.	Flies carry disease.
	Parasites cause malaria.
This poem should be read aloud.	
	My uncle owns the tractor.
A voice was heard in the distance.	
	You have to re-write your story.
He was stopped by the police.	

➢ Refer to *English for Melanesia*, Book 1, Chapter 5.

Indicator: identify what they already know about a topic and generate questions for research that will add to this information.

What do we need to do to find out information? We need to know a little bit about the topic already and then we can ask questions.

Activity 5: Questions to help you find out information

➢ Revise question words and word order as needed.

➢ The topic of LLG was chosen because LLGs are found throughout PNG.

➢ Students should be able to answer these questions if a group pools their knowledge.

➢ Answers should be compared with other groups.

➢ Students may be able to answer the second group of questions as well, but if not they should think of where to find out the answers.

➢ **Finding information**

- A small pamphlet was produced by the Department of Provincial and Local Government Affairs in 1997: *Information Pamphlet on Local-level governments under the Reforms.*
- Staff at the district office could be approached.
- A councillor or the president could be asked to speak to the class.
- Students could interview council members.
- The local Open Electorate member could be approached for information.

For you to try

Step 1

➢ The topic must be one that students can find information about without too much difficulty. If information is not available, the exercise will lose its interest for them. A topic of local interest is best, for example: coffee production—care of trees; fishing for sale—types, restrictions, markets; malaria; HIV/AIDS.

Step 2

➢ Activate latent knowledge. By asking the right questions, students realise they know something about the topic.

Step 3

➢ The above questions will reveal what they do not know about the topic. Questions are then designed to lead them to information about the topic.

Step 4

➢ Reference books, government publications, interviews etc.

➢ Example: Questions for areas where malaria is common.

1. How often has each member of your group had malaria?
2. Where do you go for help when you have malaria?
3. What treatment have members of your group had for malaria?
4. Do you know any traditional ways of treating malaria?
5. What do members of your group do to avoid getting malaria?
6. Do you know any traditional ways of avoiding malaria?
7. What are some other ways to avoid getting malaria that you know about?

8. What are some other ways of treating malaria that you know about?

Indicator: scan longer and more demanding texts to locate specific information quickly and accurately for inclusion in their own notes.

- Discuss the illustration and the idea of reading without reading every word. This is a different technique of reading. The student has a specific purpose. They should look only for the information they want and not attempt to read all the text.
- **Finding a fact you need—Scanning**
- Scanning involves a search for specific information. The student needs to form a question and then seek the answer. They need to develop the skill of forming an idea of what they are looking for, then allowing their eyes to drift or scan over a page to locate that information and no other information. The specific information can be a single fact, or a series of facts needed for project writing.

Step 1

- Teacher can think of other locally relevant examples to practise the skill.

Step 2

- There may be more than one date in the passage. A quick check is necessary to find out if it is the specific information the student wants.

Activity 7: Try some scanning

- Students do not need to answer the questions.

For you to try

- Make sure students know exactly what they are meant to do. Get the students to cover the passage of text, while you discuss the questions. They need to be sure of what they are looking for. You could set a time limit. Remind them *not* to read the text. They can do that later, for interest.
- Question 1
- Look for a number which is an age. **Two 5-year-old passengers**
- Question 2
- Look for a name of a person. **Geoff Strother**
- Now try again
- Question 1
- Look for a number of years **They can live up to 40 years**
- Question 2
- Look for a number with speed information (MPH—miles per hour) **Over 100 mph**
- Question 3
- Look for a place name. **Kimbe Bay**
- Question 4
- Look for a name joined to the word dolphin. **Spinner dolphins**

For you to try

- Writing scanning questions
- Examples:
- When were pigs introduced to the Highlands?
- When was sweet potato introduced into the Highlands?
- What did people eat before that?
- What happened after sweet potato was introduced?
- ***This technique can be practised at any time you want pupils to find facts quickly, for example, in Social Science. The only way to actually improve their reading speed and information location skills is to constantly practise.***

Indicator: skim to gain an overall sense of a complex text and write a summary.

Activity 8: Read about Kia and Minia

- Students should discuss the difference between the two stories and understand that skimming and scanning will save them from wasting time reading irrelevant facts.
- This is a vital skill for reading and note-taking for project work and factual essays. Pupils need to be able to distinguish between the main points and the details and to avoid reading a lot of unimportant detail. The first exercise shows how we don't need to read every word in order to understand something.

Activity 9: How much do we need to read?

- Students should see that there are a lot of 'padding' words in any text. The fast reader skips these and focuses on the main words.
- Full text
- **Informal Business Helping City Dwellers**
- Many young people are engaged in the informal business sector to earn money to support their parents.
- Eleven-year-old George is a shoe mender in Mount Hagen. He says he makes K30 to K40 a day to help his parents meet the cost of living in the city. He spends half of the money to buy soap, firewood, kerosene and food.
- When his family moved into the city they found life different from the village and it was hard to survive without any form of income. So George learnt to mend shoes and started out on his own.
- He urged city authorities to leave them alone. 'We are not stealing from people. We are earning an honest living.'

The National, 14 May 2003

For you to try

- Students can return to the article on sweet potato and do a skimming exercise:
- *Step 1*: Read the title and think about what will be in the article.
- *Step 2*: Have a quick look through the article to see how it is set out. Are there any headings that will help you?
- *Step 3*: Look to see if the article is divided into paragraphs.
- *Step 4*: Read the introduction. The introduction should tell you what information the article will give you. *Pupils should talk about where kaukau is planted, how long it takes to be ready to eat, etc.*
- *Step 5*: Think of some useful questions to focus your reading. *When was it introduced? Where did it come from? How did it get here? What did people eat before there was kaukau? Did people live in the Highlands then? What changes did it bring?*
- *Step 6:* Now skim read the rest of the article. Remember that the first sentence of a paragraph should tell you what the paragraph is about. *Emphasise that pupils are* not *to read the article from beginning to end.* When you find important points, slow down and read carefully. Then take notes on the important points.
- *Step 7:* Write a summary.

For you to try

- The challenge for the teacher and the students is *not* to read the article. It is hard to convince pupils that they do not need to read every word in order to understand the main points about something.
- The article has headings and the first sentences of each paragraph contain the most important information. Set a time limit depending on the ability of your class. The summary should consist of the most important information from the introduction (two sentences); the headings of each section written as a sentence; followed by a sentence of explanation (total 12 sentences).
- *The following steps prepare the pupil for reading. Discuss each step before they begin.*

Step 1

- The title clearly states the topic.

Step 2

- Yes, the article is divided into sections with headings. Some words in the headings are difficult. Explain them at this point.

Step 3

- This is not always true, but in this article pupils will find topic sentences.

Step 4

- Pupils can read all the introduction, but should then begin skimming.

Step 5

- Stress again that the idea is *not* to read every word.

Activity 11: Writing a summary

- The summary should have 12 sentences. Give the summary a title.
- Do not allow students to copy sentences from the passage. They must put the ideas in their own words.
- Sample summary. The main ideas can expressed in different words.
- Title: Help for Disabled
- Mt Sion is a centre for the disabled in the Eastern Highlands. It gives many kinds of help to disabled people. There is a hostel for 17 blind children. The children come from different parts of PNG. There is a centre for Braille. Here books are made to help blind children read. There is a hostel for deaf children. They have their own class at the Scared Heart School at Faniufa. Many people are helped by the Edmund Rice Eye and Ear Clinic and Optical Workshop. When people need glasses or hearing aids they can get them from Mt Sion. A rehabilitation program helps the disabled in the villages. They can learn life skills to make their life easier.

Activity 12: More about factual style and Activity 13: Impersonal style

- Use the longer articles to discuss personal and impersonal style. Personal style allows a little of the author to creep in—for example, in *When Pig met Potato!* the reader can tell that the author was personally interested in the subject. The article on Mt Sion is more impersonal. There are no opinions or feelings expressed. The article presents facts in an organised way.
- Have the students find similar articles themselves, from *Paradise* magazine or from the newspapers. They will also find this style in textbooks for other subjects and reference books.

Indicator: read and understand how authors acknowledge their sources.

Activities 14 and 15: Sources

- This is a skill that should be introduced gradually. In the course of looking for facts, pupils will copy information and ideas from books or magazines. You can begin to teach pupils that it is good to copy but they must say where they got the information and facts from. The information and facts belong to the book and the author of the book. You can use them, but you have to say that you used someone else's material.
- There are many conventions for acknowledging or citing material as reference. These can be slowly introduced. At this stage, students can put sources in brackets after the used material.

Student Book Chapter 7
Ways to look at the things you read

7.2.3 Interpret and explain how cultural identity, knowledge and experiences of different authors influence the responses and understanding of the audience.

Sub-strand: Contexts and texts refer to the importance of learning and using language in different situations and the fact that how we communicate influences the kind of text we use.

Three stories and three poems are given in the chapter. Teachers should find other stories and poems that can be used to reinforce the skills.

Indicator: identify personal responses to a narrative and suggest how the author achieved them.

Activity 1: Read this story and Activity 2: Vocabulary activity

- Some Maori words are used in the story, but the context should be clear. If there are any other words that the students are unfamiliar with, let them look in the dictionary.
- Ask students to discuss how this story relates to their own culture.

Activity 3: Read this story and Activity 4: Vocabulary activity

- The story of *Kiundu* is like a fable. It tells how a person's name can become the description of a personal characteristic. Proverbs are part of this culture. One is given in the story. 'It is well said that a traveller does not leave a yam roasting.' Ask students to discuss how this proverb and the story related to their own culture. Do they have similar proverbs?

Activity 5: Feelings about the story *Karanga*, Activity 6: Feelings abut the story *Kiundu* and Activity 7: Feelings about stories

- The questions are designed to help students respond personally to the stories. All answers should be accepted as long as they can be connected to the stories. Students' answers will vary. Stress that explanation of answers is important and expected, so that students will realise that they must be able to justify their responses.

Activity 8: How did the writer do it?

- Writers use techniques to influence the way we feel when we read their work. The indicator asks students to *suggest* how the author influenced them, as readers, to respond the way they did.
- Students should try to identify these techniques in the two stories. When they have identified their own personal response to the story, they should ask themselves the questions: *Why do I feel that way? What has the author done to make me feel that way?*

Indicator: propose reasons why the author chose the written ending to his/her story.

Activity 9: How stories end

- Students should identify the final stage of a narration and be able to show where the dénouement begins. The high points should be labelled according to the events in the story.
- For example, in *Karanga*, smaller high points are the grandmother giving comfort, the arrival of guests and the major high point or climax is the speech itself, the dénouement is the way the girl feels after the speech.
- Students should try to understand that the writer chose to end the story at that time and that way for a purpose and try to think what that purpose is.

Indicator: identify the narrator in a story and explain how their role and style influences the readers' point of view.

Activity 10: Who tells the story?

- Refer to *English for Melanesia,* Book 2, Chapter 11, page 112.
- The narrator of a story is revealed by the use of *I* or *he/she*. The use of *I* makes the reader feel more involved in the story as they are looking at events and feelings through the eyes of the writer. Students should try to see what the role of the narrator in each story is. Are they a participant in the story? Are they an outside observer? How does this affect the student as a reader? How does the style of the narrator affect the way you read the story? For example, the personal style of *Karanga* allows the readers to mentally step into the girl's shoes and see life through her eyes and feelings.
- 'For you to try' reveals that the point of view is important and to change it can change the way you react to a story. For example, you might feel more sympathetic to Kiundu if the story was told through his eyes (his loneliness, lack of family etc.).

Indicator: analyse a range of texts on similar themes from various cultures and compare different attitudes, beliefs and social customs.

Activity 11: Read this story and Activity 12: Culture in stories

- The cultural theme is the way in which strong customs keep a culture alive and relevant in the modern world. Each story presents different aspects of the theme.

- *Karanga* shows how the young need to be taught and to practise customs and presents this as a positive idea. The story reflects aspects of the Maori culture of New Zealand. The author is a Maori herself.
- *Kiundu* shows that acting outside your customs can lead to being isolated. It tells us many things about the culture of this group of people: that they work cooperatively, they value generosity etc. The author herself is a Kenyan.
- *The Cave of the Kopeka Bird* is a legend, so it follows the style of legends, but it still tells us about the culture of the Cook Islands—they lived in close groups, they believed in ghosts and spirits, etc. The story shows that legends can be used to illustrate and reinforce positive customary behaviour.
- Students should try to guess the meaning of words from context first, before using the dictionary.

For you to try

- Students should discuss why it is a good idea to keep customs strong. Note that customs that are outside of the laws set down by the Constitution are unlawful, even though they may be part of the culture.

Indicator: read a number of poems by the same poet, take notes and identify similarities in style or content.

Activity 13: Reading and thinking about poems and other Activities 14 to 18

- Albert Wendt was chosen because he shows a definite style in his writing. This style may confuse or put the students off at first, but they will appreciate it if given time to react to and slowly absorb meaning from the poems. He was also chosen because he has four poems in *Poetry Speaks*, a school class set. The focus of the lessons should be on style and content.
- Have a class discussion about the title of each poem before they begin reading. What do they predict from the title? What does the title say to them? For example, what do you think of when you see or hear the word 'walls'? Is it to keep something out? Is it to keep something in?
- *Lava Field and Road, Savaii*—some guiding ideas
- The poem does not contain rhythm. This reflects the subject of the poem. Lava is harsh and bleak. The images are unexpected *naked road, bleeding knees*. Why is the road *naked*? No trees, grass. *Impartial lava*—the lava of course has no feelings, does not care if your knees are bleeding. Why would the knees be bleeding—has the poet fallen? Or is this part of the way he builds up the mood? The sky is *stripped* of birds' calls—this gives a strange feeling, a silence which is wrong—and *stripped* goes back to *naked*. These images are carried on in the rest of the poem.
- *Why Can't They Stop*
- The theme of this poem is a complaint against the restrictions of custom, a rebellion against the wisdom of the old.
- *The Wall*
- This poem is a comment on the way we build imaginary walls around ourselves and cut off other people. There is also the idea that we build mental walls around things that are familiar in our society and try to keep other ideas out. Walls stop us from seeing the world as it is. Walls prevent tolerance.

Activity 14: Vocabulary activity

- The focus should be on how the poet uses the words, rather than the dictionary meaning.

Student Book Chapter 8
Different reading purposes and audiences

7.2.4 Assess the relevance, appropriateness and quality of texts in relation to purpose and audience.

Sub-strand: Critical literacy: selecting and evaluating information researched, leading to making informed choices and opinions.

The following two indicators are not dealt with specifically in the Student Book as they have been covered before. They should be covered as appropriate during the chapter.

Indicator: look up information about various topics in multiple sources and record the variations in answers given.

Indicator: read complex texts and devise concise questions necessary to clarify understanding.

Overall: Match texts with purpose and audience

For each article, poem or story in this chapter, teachers and students should discuss the relevance, appropriateness and quality of the text in relation to the audience and purpose. For example: If the audience is young children, the students should ask the following questions. Is it relevant for young children to know this? Is the topic appropriate for a young audience? Is the language appropriate for a young audience? Is the writing of good quality? Is the information given of good quality?

Activity 1: Read this article about cats, Activity 2: Who is the audience? What is the purpose? and Activity 3: Vocabulary activity

- 'Cat Community' is an informative factual article written in an informal style. The audience was probably children and the purpose to inform and entertain.
- The words which have been underlined are used to make the audience feel involved, as if they are part of the process of reading. The use of colloquial words gives an informal tone to a factual text. If students do not know other words, they should use the dictionary after they have attempted to guess meaning from context.
  - Discuss the possible audience. Is the text relevant, appropriate and of good quality for the audience?
  - Discuss the possible purpose. Is the text relevant, appropriate and of good quality for the purpose?

Activity 4: Read this poem and Activity 5: Who is the audience, what is the purpose?

- This is a poem by a well-known English poet. It is written as a song and should be read with rhythm. It is a fantasy about cats and their lives. Some of the information is the same, for example, how cats are more active at night.
- Students should be able to identify the appeal to the audience: as I said and You would say and pick out the colloquial language *airs and graces* (manners of the upper class)*; to be right* (in good condition).
  - Discuss the possible audience. Is the text relevant, appropriate and of good quality for the audience?
  - Discuss the possible purpose. Is the text relevant, appropriate and of good quality for the purpose?

Activity 6: Read this poem and Activity 7: Who is the audience, what is the purpose?

- The next poem about cats is more factual. Images of cats' lives are used. Students should note the use of contractions.
- Check students understanding of slump, plump, streak, grape, technique, creak, sneak.
- Teachers may like to comment on similarities (rhyme) and differences (rhythm) between the two poems.
  - Discuss the possible audience. Is the text relevant, appropriate and of good quality for the audience?
  - Discuss the possible purpose. Is the text relevant, appropriate and of good quality for the purpose?
- Comment on the similarities between the three texts read so far—they all give some information about cats, but they do not tell all about cats.

Activity 8: Read an article

- Read this article on cats and *For you to try*. This is a factual article about cats, with a lot of information.
- Students will read the article and make up questions that will help them understand audience and purpose.
  - Discuss the possible audience. Is the text relevant, appropriate and of good quality for the audience?
  - Discuss the possible purpose. Is the text relevant, appropriate and of good quality for the purpose?

Activity 9: Comparing audience and purpose

- Students' questions should reflect that they understand:
  - Style, amount of information given, word choice, sentence structure, punctuation and tone all reflect the writer's idea of the audience and purpose they are writing for.
  - That there is a difference between formal and informal language.
  - That formal language and informal language each have areas where they are the appropriate kind of language.
  - That language must be matched to audience and purpose, for example, technical language.
- Although all the pieces in these activities are for the audience of younger people, they have different purposes. Teachers might ask students to find other pieces of writing about cats to compare with these.
  - For fun there is a play in the *PNG School Journal* Senior 2 2004 called *A Cat for Dinner* by Florence Kiaplai.
  - Teachers should summarise with students the ideas about audience and purpose.

Indicator: write a critical appraisal of a current affairs article which is about a well known issue.

Activities 10–12 and For you to try

- This article is set out in a different way from other arguments students may have read. The point of view about the issue is built up in the article, and not clearly stated until the end.
- The death penalty is part of the law of Papua New Guinea but it has not been used. The usual punishment for murder is a long prison sentence. The question is discussed in Parliament now and then. It is an issue on which there are strong and contradictory points of view.
- A view opposing the use of the death penalty is given. Students need to critically appraise this article and decide for themselves that the point of view given has been adequately supported or not. Does it persuade you? Even if the reader does not agree or does not change their mind about the issue, they should be able to see that there are two sides to the issue and start to think about them. An argument on an issue should persuade the reader that there is another point of view.
- Students should respond to the article and should also consider their own opinion about the issue in light of what they have read in the article.

Indicator: detect half-truths or generalisations in a selection of letters to the editor.

Activity 13: Read these opinions, Activity 14: How to read letters to the editor and Activity 15: Talk about the letters

- Most letters to the editor provide opinion. There are some that give information or correct information given before. Letters to the editor often use half-truths or generalisations to make their argument stronger. However, it usually has the opposite effect and makes the argument weaker. Students should be aware of the use of *all*…instead of *some*…or *most*… when opinion is given.

Indicator: *read and consider critically two opposing views and justify own opinion with reference to passages read.*

Activity 16: Read these opposing views and Activity 17: What do you think?

- Both sides press their point of view strongly but the only 'evidence' comes from a source in the PNG E-FF statement attributed to two government departments. We do not know if this is true or if the government departments really used the words 'slave-like' which have a strong emotional effect. The Forest Minister obviously believes that large-scale logging by companies is good for PNG and the PNG E-FF does not.
- The PNG E-FF statements uses more emotive language, but the Minister uses some when he wants to put down the PNG E-FF.
- Students need to form their own opinion on the topic. They should explain how different people think in different ways and the need to assess critically any views read in the newspaper. What is in the newspaper is not necessarily the truth.
- Students could have a debate on the topic of whether PNG should continue to develop its forestry resources.
- Reference www.ecofrestry.org.pg

Indicator: *select examples from the newspaper of how opinion can sometimes be read as fact.*

- Teachers select current examples from the newspapers so that students can understand and recognise these things:
- Newspaper reports are supposed to be objective and contain facts only.
  - Reporters can give opinion, but it should be made clear to the reader that it is opinion. For example this headline *LPV system 'fool-proof'* makes it clear that 'fool-proof' is either an opinion or a quote from someone.
  - Reporters can quote the opinion of others, but the opinions must be in speech marks or clearly shown as reported speech.
  - Sometimes there are mistakes and the opinion of the reporter is made to sound like fact. These mistakes often occur when political matters are being reported.
  - Sometimes there is **bias**, for example, if a reporter supports a particular issue or political party. This can be presented as fact.
  - Make your students aware that they should always note the difference between an opinion given by the reporter (which he or she should not do) and an opinion of someone else, whom the reporter has interviewed. See this example:

> Ona to remain in hiding, *The National*, 17 July 2005
>
> A reclusive rebel leader who sparked a decade-long civil war on Bougainville...

- The description of Ona is opinion.
- Teachers should find their own examples.

Indicator: *detect bias in a written sports commentary.*

- Students began to learn about bias in Grade 6. In a sports commentary, bias would mean favouring one team over another.
- Teachers should find their own examples.

Chapter 4 Writing

About this strand

In the four chapters of this strand, students will practise activities that develop writing skills. When teaching writing skills, teachers need to keep in mind the language principles stated in the *Language Upper Primary Teachers Guide 2003*. For the writing strand, they are that the principles of writing are based on the belief that all students need opportunities to:

- write every day (as part of Language or another part of the curriculum),
- learn to write by writing (the teacher's role is not to talk about writing, but to provide many opportunities for students to do writing),
- learn to write by talking about their writing (students should discuss their writing in pairs or groups and with the teacher),
- learn to write following models of different types of genre,
- be aware of the many different contexts and purposes of writing that are used in the real world,
- see teachers using the writing process as part of their teaching,
- have their own and other class members writing displayed around them to create a 'print rich environment',
- have positive feedback about their progress in writing tasks,
- have time in the class to go through the whole process of writing without pressure to complete 'the product',
- have time in the classroom to share their completed writing with other students,
- be allowed to have some responsibility for the way their writing skills are developing (for example, if they can assess their own needs for paragraph development skills, they should be allowed to refine those skills with extra tasks),
- think about the writing process,
- write for different purposes, and
- write for real audiences (for readers outside the classroom).

based on *Language Upper Primary Teachers Guide 2003,* page 6

Two key skills and processes for teaching writing are the **writing process** and using **genres**. These are outlined in the *Language Upper Primary Teachers Guide 2003,* page 11. The students have learnt about the writing process in Grade 6. Revise this process as appropriate.

Skills in using different genres are developed in all Language strands. In the writing strand, teachers should follow the four-step process (this also applies to oral use of the genres), found on page 11 of the Guide. Activities in this four-step guide are covered in the other strands, demonstrating that writing cannot be taught in isolation.

Each chapter in the writing strand covers one of the outcomes for writing. The outcomes can be used to measure students' achievements in creating meaning in written language. The indicators are samples of the kind of activity you can use to check if the outcome has been reached. The indicators given in the syllabus have been used as a basis for activities in the Student Book. Teachers can plan other activities that also help students reach the outcomes for that chapter. Many of the writing activities are integrated with speaking and listening and reading in both Language and other subjects.

The activities and materials in the Student Book are not divided into lessons. A teacher will decide on the outcome to be taught and then select material for that outcome. Some material may be from different Language strands. The templates in the Appendix will help teachers use the Student Book and this book.

Key words

These are words that you as a teacher, and your students, will be using in the four chapters of the Writing strand (in order of use in the Student Book). You will find an explanation of the words in Appendix 6, the Glossary.

Chapter 9
reaction, record, react, personally, myth, mythical, legend, legendary, version, conventions

Chapter 10
antecedent, ambiguous, pronoun, refer, pronoun reference, metaphor, metaphorical expression, clarity, clear, concise, conciseness, refine, direct speech, indirect speech, handout, practical demonstration

Chapter 11
figurative, message, reconstruct, creative reconstruction, personification, mood, atmosphere, meaning, prose, alternative, setting

Chapter 12
commentary, focus article, evaluate, quality, slogan, superlatives, exaggeration, claim, humour, emotion

Links to other main subjects

Chapter 9
Poems, play and stories—respect and tolerance—Personal Development
The Pendant—cultural identity—Social Science

Chapter 10
Poems—ways of looking at life—Personal Development

Chapter 11
Poems and stories—ways of looking at life—Personal Development

Chapter 12
Is wantokism killing PNG?—unity, national identity, cultural identity (Activity 1 and Activity 11), Social Science, Personal Development
Reporting on women's issues—role and status of women, Social Science, Personal Development
Chief: PNG needs national dress—Social Science, Personal Development

Possible assessment tasks

The *Language Upper Primary Teachers Guide 2003* (pages 46 and 47) provides some ideas about assessing writing. The suggested areas for assessment are:

- analysis of unassisted writing samples,
- process for unassisted writing samples,
- text summaries,
- teacher-designed writing tasks,
- negotiated lists of criteria,
- journals, diaries and drafts,
- spelling checklists, and
- a general criteria sheet framework.

Teachers will assess writing across all the Language strands and other curriculum areas.

Tests for Chapter 9

Chapter 9 of the Student Book consists of examples of some kinds of writing and opportunities for students to try these kinds of writing. The examples will be kept in their writing portfolios.

For assessment in this strand, teachers will provide students with appropriate writing tasks following the examples given. When they have done the tasks, students should think about what they have learnt, and fill in the table below. Teachers can also use the tables as assessment guides. As teachers, you will use some of these things to help you know how well your students are writing, and students can see what they can do to make their writing better.

(*Note*: This table can be adjusted so that students can grade their self-assessment as good, needs improvement, etc.)

1. Ask your students to fill in this table

I am able to react to a poem or story.	
I can see that writers put their feelings into poems and stories.	
I can record my reaction.	
I can write about my reaction.	
I can use the writing process to do this.	
I can write paragraphs that have one main point which is developed in the paragraph.	
I can summarise the plot of the story so that I can put a new event in.	
I can write notes on the characters so that the character I add fits into the story.	
I understand that sometimes there is a particular purpose for taking notes.	
I can take notes for a particular purpose.	
I can use those notes to write a paragraph.	
I can identify myths and legends by their style.	
I can write in the style of myths and legends.	
I can recognise a play by the way it is set out.	
I can correctly set out a play that I have written.	
I can recognise the way stage directions are given in a play.	
I can use stage directions correctly in my own play.	
I can turn personal notes into notes for others to read.	
I can write a variety of letters that have real purposes.	

Tests for Chapter 10

Chapter 10 of the Student Book considers skills and strategies for improving areas of writing.

1. Pronouns

Correct these sentences to remove the ambiguity.

1. When Anna's mother took her to the market she sold a lot of peanuts. Anna sold

a lot of peanuts when her mother took her to the market. Her mother sold a lot of peanuts when she took Anna to the market.

2. Her mother told her she had left a mess in the kitchen. 'You have left a mess in the kitchen,' her mother told her. 'I have left a mess in the kitchen,' her mother told her.
3. Hari and his father went to Madang when he wanted to buy a bicycle. When Hari wanted to buy a bicycle, he went with his father to Madang. When his father wanted to buy a bicycle, he went to Madang with Hari.
4. Tau told Lohia he had made a mistake. 'You have made a mistake, Tau,' said Lohia. 'You have made a mistake, Lohia,' said Tau.
5. If the shoes do not fit your children, put them in the box. Put the shoes in the box if they do not fit your children.

2. Use this poem

Use this poem or another of your choice for students to:

a) add to or change;
b) turn it into a colloquial dialogue.

The Sunset by Nancy Bodema taken from OUP, The Pacific Series, *Using English*, Pupils Book 1, page 89

It cools the brains of
all things on earth and
in the sky.
It sits peacefully
to comfort every heart
from their sorrows and fears.
It throws away
the anger.
It spreads its harmless
embers all over the sky
to welcome the peaceful night.
It brightens every living thing
with its reflection.

3. Ask your students to fill in this table

I can use pronouns correctly, so that my pronoun reference is clear.	
I can see that poems have a structure.	
I can use the structure of a poem to add to it.	
I can use the structure of a poem to replace ideas in the poem with new ideas.	
I can write a dialogue using colloquial language.	

4. Create metaphors

Students create metaphors for this list of words and phrases. They must use their imagination to create fresh metaphors.

1. a bird of paradise
2. a flag
3. a sink full of unwashed dishes
4. a broken canoe
5. burnt rice
6. a dry garden
7. a PMV with a smoky exhaust
8. a yellow hibiscus
9. a fat cat
10. a clean river

5. Ask your students to fill in this table

I can see how a sports report is set out.	
I can identify a reader for my sports report.	
I can plan and write sports reports.	
I can edit and refine my writing of sports reports, especially checking for clear and concise writing.	
I can identify my reader for a handout on a skill.	
I can plan and write a summary for a handout.	
I can edit and refine my handout writing.	

Tests for Chapter 11

Chapter 11 looks how writers influence their readers.

1. A writer's influence

Write a list of things that you as a writer can do to influence the reader. Give examples from your own writing. Say what influence you wanted to have and how you carried that out in your writing.

2. **Identify these types of figurative language:** metaphor, simile, personification. Say what is being compared in each sample. Analyse the effectiveness of the sample—is it appropriate and believable, is it fresh or stale? *Sample answers—students may have other ideas.*

Sample	*Type*	*Comparison*	*Effectiveness*
Their dresses are green and pink orchids	*metaphor*	*colour of dresses and colour of orchids*	*fresh image, comparison is clear*
The blood leaked from the mountain's wounds.	*personification*	*blood from a wound with water from a landslide or stream*	*striking image, appropriate to poem*
The sun lies down on the floor.	*personification*	*sun with animal, e.g., cat or person basking in the sun*	*clear, fresh idea of restful time warm in the sun*
He eats like a greedy pig.	*simile*	*greedy person and pig (known as greedy eaters)*	*clear but not fresh*
The mosquito's body is a mini-blood bank.	*metaphor*	*body of mosquito holding blood like a blood bank (Red Cross)*	*clear, striking, appropriate*
Lightning danced around the room.	*personification*	*rapidly moving light and dancing person*	*clear, could be more striking, and more original*
The sun stretched its golden arms down from the sky.	*personification*	*arms of person and rays of sun*	*clear but not fresh*
The waves nibbled at the beach with their sharp teeth.	*personification*	*waves eating away at beach, teeth*	*clear, could be more striking*
You are as slow as a tortoise.	*simile*	*slow person, slow animal*	*stale*
The coconut frond fanned the sky.	*personification*	*person using fan, coconut branch*	*clear, fresh*

3. Ask your students to fill in this table

I recognise that there are many ways a writer can influence their audience.	
I recognise there are many reasons why a writer tries to influence their audience.	
I understand that writers appeal to the readers' sympathies in the language they use.	
I understand that writers can have a message they want to give to the reader.	
I understand the role of figurative language in influencing the reader.	
I can use different kinds of language to give a message to my reader.	
I can use different kinds of language to influence my reader.	
I know how to use figurative language.	
I understand that a writer has a purpose in choosing to end the story in the way he has written it.	
When I write my own stories, I plan the ending to fit the story and to give the message I want the reader to understand.	
I can use mood to create meaning in my writing.	
I understand I have to give the reader enough information to create meaning in my writing.	

4. Further assessment

If teachers need further assessment, they should ask students to write a special piece that covers message, influence, meaning, mood and atmosphere.

Tests for on Chapter 12

Chapter 12 of the Student Book looks at some skills for writing persuasion, such as using superlatives. These can be assessed by the following activity. Other skills require similar kinds of activities as are given in the chapter, such as students analysing a passage for its persuasive devices and successfully using persuasive devices themselves.

Teachers should collect articles which can be *adapted* for students. The 'Focus' section of the *Post-Courier* is a good source of discussion on relevant and current issues. Choose articles that have mostly opinion to demonstrate emotive language, and some which have statistics to show how facts can be used in persuasion.

Students can be asked, for example, to write about an issue using comic exaggeration. (Choose your issue carefully—some are just not suitable, such as AIDS or domestic violence.)

1. Using superlatives

Copy these sentences and put different superlatives in the spaces.

1. The __________________ bicycle in Lae!
2. Kokomo Washing Powder is __________________ to your clothes.
3. Buy Four X bread, it is the __________________ .
4. Travel to New Ireland, the __________________ Province!
5. ZigZag Bilum Rope, the __________________ .

Students can use *the ......est, most ....* or *irregular forms*, such as best.

2. Ask your students to fill in this table

I can tell when a text is meant to persuade (its purpose is to persuade).	
I can tell who the writer meant his audience to be.	
I can identify the main point of a persuasive text.	
I can draw up a plan of a persuasive text to show the main point and how it is supported.	
I can tell the difference between fact and opinion in a persuasive text.	
I can recognise the way a writer uses emotive words to persuade.	
I can recognise the way a writer uses exaggeration to persuade.	
I can recognise the way a writer uses an appeal to the reader to persuade.	
I can recognise that a writer can use humorous style to persuade.	
I can recognise the way a writer uses half-truths and generalisations to persuade.	
I can write a persuasive text that uses fact, opinion and persuasive devices.	
I can recognise the language that is used in advertisements.	
I can use persuasive language to write an advertisement.	

Teacher information

In this section you will find information on the activities and background to some activities in the four chapters of the Writing strand. The information is for you to use, if you wish, in helping you plan your lessons.

The *Language Upper Primary Teachers Guide 2003* (pages 28–31) provides writing strategies for the teacher to use in teaching writing. These can be applied to the activities in the Student Book. The topics covered are dictagloss, journal writing and paragraph writing (including grammar).

Students should use the writing process for all writing tasks given (see Teachers Resource Book,

Grade 6) and keep all examples of writing in a writing portfolio.

You will find the answers to Student Book Activities in Appendix 5.

Student Book Chapter 9
Writing for different audiences and purposes

7.3.1 Plan and produce a range of more complex literary and factual texts for a broad range of purposes and audiences.

Sub-strand: Production—to provide opportunities for students to use language for real purposes.

Indicator: record ideas, reflections and predictions about a story or poem.

Activities 1 to 6 and For you to try

- Reading texts, questions about texts, reactions to texts
- A poem contains many thoughts and suggestions. Often the topics are outside the students' experiences. If we ask students to *explain* a poem they may have problems. If they are asked to *react* instead, their understanding will increase. This reaction can come through activities, such as turning the play into a role play or an interview.
- Poetry is 'reactional' language to make people react personally to other people's way of seeing things. It contrasts with 'interactional' language, such as conversation, and 'transactional' language, such as giving instructions or giving an opinion.
- Poems give us other people's way of seeing things—people, landscapes, animals, happy events, sad events and so on.
- Choose poems that are within the students' range of experiences, but stretch them a little.
- Reaction to a poem is a very personal thing. Students should be working individually and allowed to come up with their own reactions—you may get a range of reactions—this is good. All reactions (within limits of sense) are acceptable.
- Students may not feel confident to share their reactions, so writing a paragraph gives the teacher a chance to read or hear each student's individual response. If the students are confident they can have a group discussion about the various reactions.

Indicator: write a new character or event into a story, maintaining the author's style and using paragraphs to organise and develop detail.

For you to try

1. The new **event** must fit into the story. In order to fit the new event in smoothly, the student will need to analyse the plot.
2. The new **character** must fit into the story. Before writing, students will need to analyse the present characters and make up their own character that will react with those characters in an appropriate way. Tell students that characters are defined by the author by:
   speech: what they say and how they speak or think,
   others: what other people say about them,
   action: what they do,
   appearance: their facial expressions and gestures, what they look like.
3. The writer's **style**: If the writing is formal then the student must use formal writing. If it is very descriptive, then the students' writing should be the same etc.

- Revise paragraph construction. Revise dialogue paragraphs—a new paragraph for each new person speaking. Revise dialogue punctuation.

Indicator: make notes for different purposes and build on these notes in own writing or speaking.

Activity 7: Read this article and Activity 8: Take notes on this article

- Students must decide on the purpose before they begin taking notes. Notes should only be taken on parts of the article relevant to their chosen purpose. Purposes could be:
  - you are introducing a new perfume called *Frangi*,

- you want to persuade the council to plant frangipani in the streets,
- you are giving a talk on the kind of plants found in the botanical gardens, or
- you want to write a book on the origin of common flower trees in PNG.

Activity 9: Write up your notes

➢ The paragraphs must suit the chosen purpose and audience.

Indicator: plan and write own versions of legends and myths using structures identified in reading.

Activity 10: Reading and writing myths and legends and For you to try

➢ *English for Melanesia,* Book 1, Chapters 10 and 11 cover this topic and provide additional activities.

➢ Myths and legends are not always differentiated in traditional stories. The two legends, for example, have mythical elements.

➢ Legend and legendary are used more loosely today—often sports heroes are called legends.

➢ Structures students should use include:

- myths usually begin with 'once upon a time',
- setting and characters (not always human) are described,
- in myths the question to be answered must be clear,
- the answer should be magical,
- in legends there needs to be a clear heroic character who does some deed that is remembered in the legend,
- the language is descriptive, and
- there is clear narrative plot.

Indicator: write own one-act play script, applying some of the conventions learnt from reading, including production notes.

Activities 11–12 and For you to try

Reading a play and questions about the play

➢ The play has a moral and can lead to discussion about the character of Nasrudin. He appears to be an honest man, but is he?

Activity 13: How to write plays

Conventions

➢ Stages are described by *up* (away from the audience), *down* (close to the audience), *left* and *right* as seen from the audience. It is a good idea to have students draw a plan of the stage and put in any props that would be on the stage.

➢ Plays are written in a recognisable format. In the sample play, the narrator gives some of the stage directions, while other stage directions are given in brackets or italic type.

➢ The characters, props and stage setting are given at the beginning.

➢ The play can be an adaptation of a story in this book or other short stories. Students can act out the play.

Indicator: convert personal notes into notes for others to read, paying attention to appropriateness of style, vocabulary and presentation.

➢ This is revision of formal/informal language.

➢ Put up a personal note on the board and ask students to note the features:
I'll be late. Scrape two coconut. Big ones. Thanks.

Features:

- grammatical errors (coconuts)
- sentence fragments (big ones)
- colloquial language (thanks)
- contractions (I'll)
- telegraphic style—short sentences with some words missing.

➢ Now ask students to change the note as if it was written to a visitor to your house, that is, in a more formal style.
I am sorry I will be late. If you like, you could scrape the two large coconuts in the cupboard under the sink. Thank you.

Indicator: draft and write individual, group or class letters and telecommunications for real purposes.

➢ Students have learnt something about letter writing in Grade 6. *English for Melanesia,* Book 2, Chapter 3 covers the topic.

➢ Find an appropriate occasion for real life letters to be written.

Student Book Chapter 10
Improve your writing skills

7.3.2 Apply a broad range of skills and strategies to define their own more complex writing and that of others.

Sub-strand: Skills and Strategies acknowledging the importance of skills and strategies necessary to effectively communicate.

Indicator: review and edit own writing to produce a final form, matched to the needs of an identified reader.

- Teachers should emphasise the editing and refining part of the writing process during this chapter and the following chapters.
- The reader/audience should be identified before the writing process begins. Editing for an 'identified reader' means looking at all the aspects of audience they have learnt about so far, to check that they have matched their writing to the language needs, age, information needs etc. to that identified reader.

Indicator: record and acknowledge sources in own writing.

- Students have learnt some ideas about acknowledging sources in Chapter 6. Revise what they know and show some examples.

Students should acknowledge sources in this chapter and the following chapters. For example, any poem they use in the Indicator: *use structures of poems read to write additional verses or substitution of ideas*, should be acknowledged to the author and the source of the poem, such as *Poetry Speaks*. They can put (adapted by <u>**own name**</u>) as part of the title. If they do some research before writing their handout for a process, they must acknowledge the source. For example, the frangipani perfume process comes from page 308, *Liklik Buk: A Sourcebook for Development Workers in Papua New Guinea,* 1986, Unitech, PMB Lae. They do not need to be able to reference using all these details. A student reference at this level could be *Liklik Buk*, page 308.

Poetry Speaks should be referred to like this (if the student adapted the poem 'The Eagle'):

'The Eagle', by Alfred Lord Tennyson, *Poetry Speaks*, Leone Peguero and Ganga Powell, Heinemann Educational Australia Pty Ltd, 1988, page 34, adapted by <u>**own name**</u>.

Indicator: ensure pronouns clearly indicate to what and to whom they refer.

Activity 1: Making your pronouns clear and For you to try

- Revise pronoun types if necessary.
- Pronouns *refer* (go back to) to nouns or noun phrases called *antecedents*. The antecedents control what pronoun is used. If the right pronouns are not used there can be ambiguity and confusion in the pronoun reference. Activity 1 highlights this possible confusion. But it is more important for students to:
  a) know that it can occur, and
  b) make sure they check for it when editing their work, and make necessary adjustments.
- Questions to ask to help students with Activity 1. There is often more than one way to grammatically correct such sentences. Students should pick the most likely.
  1. Who shouted, Hannah or her sister?
  2. Who had a good time, Tau or his cousin?
  3. Who is going bald, Gabi or his father?
  4. What broke, the dish or the bucket?
  5. Did A team or B team win? Not clear, make a choice.
  6. Do we lock up the children or lock up the cupboard?
  7. Who won, Kafa or Mubi? Not clear, make a choice.
  8. Who did the headmaster ask to see, Safira or Luci? Not clear, make a choice.
  9. Was it Agata or her mother who got married?
  10. Who was the student at the time, Manuia or Poro? Not clear, make a choice.

Indicator: use colloquialisms in written dialogue.

Activity 2: Dialogue writing and For you to try

- Students should work together and identify the colloquial language (e.g., *Long time*

Writing

meaning *It's a long time since I saw you last*). They should also note informal language, such as ungrammatical sentences and contractions (e.g., *I'm*).

- The following colloquial expressions may be unfamiliar to your students. Allow them to attempt an explanation from context first, before explaining if necessary.
  - living from hand to mouth—live in poverty
  - to let the cat out of the bag—tell what should be kept secret
  - feather in your cap—something to be proud of.
- Students now write their own dialogue. They can use colloquial expressions they learnt about in Chapter 4.
- Students should decide who is going to hear/read the dialogue (identify their readers/listeners) and write and edit with those readers/listeners in mind.

Indicator: use structures of poems read to write additional verses or substitution of ideas.

Activities 3–5 and For you to try

- Students should read the poems aloud in pairs.
- They should also read their poems aloud when they have added to or changed them.

Activity 6: Choosing your words in poems and For you to try

- A poet's choice of words is very personal. A poet may re-write a poem many times. Students can choose any word which fit the sense, rhyme and feelings of the poem. Here is the published version.

First Dip

Wave after wavelet goes
Coldly over your toes
And sinks down into the stones.
Another mounts to your knees,
Icy, as if to freeze
Flesh, marrow and bones.
And now another, a higher
Yellow with foam, and dire
With weeds from yesterday's storm.
With a gasp you greet it—
Your shoulders stoop to meet it—
And you find, you find,
Ah-h-h!
You find the water's warm!

John Walsh

Indicator: investigate metaphorical expressions and create own where appropriate.

Activity 7: Metaphors and Activity 8: Match the metaphor

- Students should build on their knowledge of similes. Metaphors are similes without the words 'as' and 'like'. Metaphors are used in everyday speech as well as literature.
- Ask them to think of metaphors they use themselves.
- Encourage students to think of original, fresh and striking metaphors. Over-used metaphors become worn out and like clichés. For example, *he climbed the ladder to success*. Over-used metaphors are acceptable in everyday speech, but not in writing. In everyday speech we do not have time to stop and think of fresh metaphors when we want to make comparisons in this way, but we should take the time when writing.
- As well as locating the metaphors in Activity 7, they should look for metaphors in other poems as in this book or other books, and make a collection of those that appeal to them.

For you to try

- *Poetry Speaks*, pages 78 and 79, has some good examples of two-line images. Chapter 7 in *Poetry Speaks* deals with images in poems.
- Students can also turn poems into prose writing, keeping the metaphors.
- Refer also to *English for Melanesia*, Book 1, Chapter 16.

Indicator: plan, create, edit and refine short sports match reports and focus on clarity and conciseness.

Activities 9–12 and For you to try

- *Questions*: Reports, sports or otherwise follow an upside-down pyramid shape, with the most important information coming first, then less important, and then information which is not so important or may just be some background fact at the end.
- Teachers and students can find sports reports that interest them to use for this indicator. Stress the need for writing for an identified reader.
- Refer to *English for Melanesia*, Book 1, Chapter 20.

Indicator: prepare an expressive handout to accompany a practical demonstration of a skill or hobby.

Activities 13–14 and For you to try

- Encourage students to do research or to find out about traditional processes. If they use a written or oral source, these must be acknowledged.
- Stress the need for writing for an identified reader.

Student Book Chapter 11
Making choices in your writing

7.3.3 Assess how well own writing presents meaning and how effective this is in influencing the audience.

Sub-strand: Context and Text refers to the importance of learning and using language in different situations and the fact that how we communicate influences the kind of text we use.

Indicator: compare features of two pieces of own writing and discuss how they could influence the reader.

Activity 1: Read this story, Activity 2: How well does writing present meaning? and For you to try

- Students will probably say the writer aimed to show that it is good to have dreams. The message is that dreams do not have to be clearly defined, as long as you realise that it is possible for you to have them. The writer gets his message across by making you sympathise with and understand the characters.
- After analysing how the story *I Wanna Be* has influenced them, students should look at their own work to assess how well their own writing presents meaning and whether it is effective in the way it influences their audience.

Indicator: use different forms of figurative language to create mood or atmosphere then present to group or class and note responses.

Indicator: produce poetry through revision by deleting or adding words or reorganising words or lines, experimenting with images through figurative language.

- *Figurative language* is defined in a number of ways, such as: metaphorical language; words used not in the literal sense but in an imaginative way or way different from their usual meaning (a *fiery* man). Students have already read and used figurative language. The most common figurative language uses are metaphors, similes and personification.
- *Personification* is giving live characteristics to an inanimate (not part of the animal world) object, such as the house 'waits' or giving human characteristics to animals.
- In addition there is the use of a figurative meaning rather than literal meaning as defined above (*the computer in his head*—his brain) and the exploitation of multiple meanings of words.
- Students should find and list all the examples of figurative language in Activities 3 to 6 and For you to try.

Activity 3: Pictures with words

- The description and the poem both use figurative language.
- Teachers will need to explain *mood* and *atmosphere*.

Activity 4: Read a poem with personification

Personification

- Identify the personification in the poem.

For you to try

- Do some writing with personification. Emphasise the need for originality to add interest and colour to writing.

Activity 5: Being creative with language

Ideas from Alan Maley and Alan Duff, *The Inward Ear, Poetry in the classroom*, Cambridge, 1989: 1. Adapted from *Jungle*, *The Pacific Series, Using English*, Grade 6, Book1, page 121. 2. Adapted from Keats, *Ode on Melancholy*.

- Students discuss each choice in groups then as a group read their poem aloud.
- Class discussion can follow to reach agreement on the best choice.

Activity 6: A paragraph from a poem and Activity 7: A poem from a paragraph

- Students practise writing figurative language.

For you to try

- Students write a poem and a descriptive passage with figurative language.
- This will be presented to the class and students should note responses—they can do this by asking questions.

Indicator: draw illustrations from own written text and consider whether the text conveys sufficient information to create setting or mood for the reader.

Activities 8–10

- The mood in the story begins with confusion, goes on to fear and being worried, frightened, then relieved when the pendant is found, understanding of the role of the pendant in her life, and happiness that her first worry about the uniform was solved.

Indicator: write an alternative ending for a known story and discuss in groups how this would change the characters or alter the outcome of the story.

Activity 11: Change the ending and Activity 12: What does changing the ending mean?

- Discuss 'outcome', 'alternative' and 'alter' with class.
- Remind the students that the author had a certain outcome in mind, something she wanted to tell the reader. And now they are changing this. So they must think what they want the outcome to be, what they have in mind for the characters.

For you to try

- Students should write a story that has both mood and setting.
- They should share their story with a group and listen to the ideas of other students. They need to think about whether they have given enough information in their writing to create a setting or mood for the reader.
- Students can also go back to any other stories they have written and find (*draw*) examples (*illustrations*) from those texts to think about (*consider*) if they have given enough (*sufficient*) information to the reader to create setting or mood.

Student Book Chapter 12 Writing effective persuasion

7.3.4 Assess the relevance, appropriateness and quality of own writing in relation to the purpose and audience.

Sub-strand: Critical Literacy acknowledges that language learners and users need to think beyond content and recognise and evaluate the beliefs that influence texts.

Indicator: evaluate own and a range of texts for persuasiveness, clarity and quality of information.

Indicator: identify bias, prejudice and half-truths in writing.

Indicator: distinguish between opinion and fact in writing.

Activities 1–6 and For you to try commentaries and discussion

- The indicators ask students to look at texts written by others and their own texts. The first six activities are focused on other writer's texts to allow students to analyse as a group. In 'For you to try' they are given a topic, but teachers can provide a different topic which is more relevant to their students. They should look as critically at their own writing as they did at that of others. The finished writing can be shared in a group of with the class and evaluated in terms of persuasiveness, clarity and quality. Quality is not covered in the activities. This means to make a judgement based on your own perspective of what are good style, taste and value. These are judgements which are developed over time.
- Students can also answer these questions for the article in Activity 11.
- Refer to *English for Melanesia,* Book 1, Chapter 21 'Opinions in newspapers'.
- Refer to *English for Melanesia,* Book 2, Chapter 19 'Communication by advertising'.

Activities 7–10 and For you to try Advertising

- Persuasion in advertising is a more open kind of persuasion. It has a clear purpose of persuading someone to do something, such as buy or use.
- Provide real advertisements for students to analyse. Collect those that illustrate the ideas in the chapter.
- Refer to *English for Melanesia,* Book 2, Chapter 19 'Communicating with advertising'.

Indicator: investigate in detail the use of persuasive devices in writing, for example, words and phrases, humour, emotion and ambiguity.

Activity 11: Read this article, Activity 12: Talk about the article, and For you to try

- Revise sympathy and empathy, emotive language.

Activity 14: Read this passage

- The style of the passage is 'comic exaggeration'. It can be very effective because it makes the reader relate to the writer.

Activity 17: Using emotion in persuasion

- Emotional appeals in an argument can be made by:
  - the way the writer selects examples and illustrations,
  - word choice, for example, to say someone is *careful with money* is positive, but *mean with money* is negative, and
  - metaphor—favourable or unfavourable (*poison to the economy/medicine to the economy*). You could ask students to think of favourable and unfavourable metaphors for a list of classes of people, such as politician, betelnut sellers, PMV drivers etc.

Indicator: analyse the message of a modern song and evaluate the effectiveness of music and rhythm to communicate its meaning.

- Have students note the words of a song that appeals to them and contains a message for the modern world. They can present an argument that the song is effective in highlighting the issue.

Summary activity For you to try

- Discuss and list on the board all that has been learnt about writing good persuasion, such as using emotive words, metaphors, giving facts etc.

Appendices

Appendix 1: Lesson planning table

Outcomes	Things to work from and plan for
1. Learning outcome	Identify the outcome in the curriculum that you are working from.
2. Content: topic or key concept	Base this on the outcome. Decide on a theme, from other curriculum areas if appropriate, for example, our local culture.
3. What will learners learn in the particular lessons?	How will learners achieve the learning outcome? • what knowledge will they learn? • what skills will they learn? • what values and attitudes will they adopt?
4. Number of lessons that need to be taught	How many lessons do you plan to teach on this particular topic?

Assessing progress	Things to think through
1. Evidence of learning	What you will look for in each learner's work? Write down the assessment objectives. (Each one should be something a learner can do.)
2. The way learning will be assessed	Examples of what procedures you may use: • formal (oral or written presentation) • informal (teacher observation) • small task within a larger project • homework • test

Classroom practice	Things to consider
1. Method or activity	What will you do and what will learners do, and in what sequence?
2. Time	For how long will you explain or model new concepts? For how long will learners do each activity?
3. Teaching methods	How exactly will you arrange learners? • as a whole group? • working in pairs? • working individually?
4. Resources needed	Where will learners be? • in the classroom? • outside? List any resources you may need for students to complete tasks.

Appendix 2: Yearly plan

Units of work	Term 1	Term 2	Term 3	Term 4
Speaking and listening	Outcome… Indicator…			
Reading				
Writing				

Appendix 3: Term plan

Week	Outcomes	Student tasks	Required resources	Assessment procedures
1–3				
4–6				
7–10				

Appendix 4: Lesson plan

Teaching group √	Required Materials
Individual Whole class Team group	
Learning Strategies	**Specific Content—lesson plan Collaborating**
Interpreting Predicting Planning √ Investigating Recording √ Justifying Changing Communicating √	
Curriculum Strand	**Assessment strategy**
Cross Curricula Strands	**Cross Curricula activities**

Appendix 5: Answers to activities in the Student Book

Student Book Chapter 1

Activity 4: Another issue

1. There are several issues in the letter. Students can choose one of those listed (public health and public safety, laws not being used, people with no jobs, good nutrition) or come up with another issue.
2. The writer is arguing that street selling causes problems.
3. The letter argument only shows the negative side. There are many positive points about street selling.

Activity 7: Kinds of questions

Question types	*Example(s) from role play*
a) questions beginning with question words	How can we go against it? (7)
b) questions beginning with verbs	(3) Will the husband's family be paying bride price? (6) Is a woman really something we should pay for?
c) false questions (that have already been answered)	(1) Is she? The question has already been answered by Tagua's first statement. This is something we do in dialogue to show we are listening and responding. (8) Do you? The question has already been answered by Tagua's statement *I agree with Hannah.*
d) questions that are tagged onto the end of a statement (question tags)	(5) It will have to be done soon, wont' it? (10) It's a social issue, isn't it?
e) negative questions	(4) Doesn't it need to be settled first? These questions begin with a negative verb. The word order is the same as positive verb questions.
f) questions that read like a statement, but end with a question mark	(2) She went to the village already? We only know this is a question because of the question mark. The student should try to read it without the question mark. They will see that it is a statement grammatically, but in the dialogue the tone of voice makes it into a question. (9) We could use this issue for our role play? Repeat the process as for Question (2).

Activity 8: More about question tags

Statement with a negative verb	*Tag with a positive verb*
The people haven't agreed about bride price,	have they?
It isn't right to pay bride price in the city,	is it?
Your cousin doesn't want to get married,	does she?
The man doesn't really know her,	does he?
The won't move to the village,	will they?

Statement with a positive verb	*Tag with a negative verb*
The people have agreed about bride price,	haven't they?
It is clear that they must hurry up,	isn't it?
Your cousin wants to get married,	doesn't she?
The man knows her well,	doesn't he?
They will move to the village,	won't they?

Activity 12: Asking questions about the commentary

1. Madang
2. Eastern Highlands
3. 45%
4. Western Highlands (at risk)
5. Eastern Highlands

Activity 13: Giving answers with details

Suggested answers:

1. No, the Eastern Highlands has the lowest percentage of girls of total enrolment, but also the lowest percentage of girls at risk of dropping out. In the Western Highlands where the percentage of girls enrolled is the same as the average, 77% of girls are at risk of dropping out.
2. The risk of girls dropping out in Madang (50%) is lower than the average of 65%. However, it is clear that girls are at risk of not completing their education.
3. Yes, the two provinces that had help from UNICEF, Western Highlands and Simbu, especially Simbu, showed high rates of re-enrolment. *The teacher could point out that this figure is thus artificial and not sustainable.*
4. Madang (16%) and Morobe (16%) have low percentages of girls dropping out, but they also have very low percentages of girls re-enrolling (Madang 6%, Morobe 4%). This contrasts with East Sepik (14%) where there is a low percentage of girls dropping out but a high percentage of girls re-enrolling (58%).

Student Book Chapter 2

Activity 3: Talking about the two passages

1. Passage 1—to honour a special day. Passage 2—to report on and give feelings about a special day.
2. Passage 1—important people, the people of PNG. Passage 2—readers of the newspaper.
3. It is the sort of language used in public speeches that are designed to inspire and uplift, e.g., 'This is the end of an era and the beginning of another'.
4. The first paragraph is factual reporting; in the second paragraph the author allows his emotions to show.

Activity 4: Adapting language

1. But how did you live in the bush for that time? Question beginning with question word (But) how….
2. How could you cook food? Question beginning with question word.
3. Wouldn't the solders see if you lit a fire? Question beginning with verb (negative question).
4. The soldiers must have been moving around in our area? Statement question.
5. What do you mean? Question beginning with question word.
6. You did? False question.
7. That's the way we go to visit Grandpa's grave, isn't it? Question tag.

Activity 14: Cause and effect

Cause/reason	*Effect/result*
Transport is the biggest problem to all activity in Papua New Guinea.	This means it is difficult for farmers to sell their goods or bring the goods from the towns to the villages.
But there are 80 000 more people joining the workforce each year.	Therefore there is no work for most of them.
Therefore there is no work for most of them.	As a result, they will have to work in the informal sector.
the informal sector needs to grow and prosper.	In order to make the economy grow,
Growth will help get the money needed	so that health service, education, farm extension services and well looked after roads are possible.
Transport will have to be improved	so that the informal sector can grow.
It is expensive to transport stuff such as chicken feed or fertiliser.	Therefore people have stopped expanding their businesses.
Agricultural extension services have been getting bad over the last 20 years.	As a result, seventy percent of the informal sector households in Central Province said they had not received any support.
Law and order is also a problem for the informal sector.	It affects people producing goods and it affects people being able to buy things when they sell their goods.

Activity 15: Making a summary

It is not true that mining and large projects will develop PNG because they do not employ many of the available workers. These workers become part of the informal sector. The informal sector could become very important in the economy, but there are constraints or problems that must be overcome.

The biggest problem is transport which adds to the costs of running an informal business.

As well, lack of services and law and order problems are holding back the rural informal sector. The challenge is to get the informal sector going strong so that it will help the economy of the future.

Title: Constraints in the rural sector		
Paragraph	*Main points*	*Development of points*
introduction	problems in rural informal sector	informal rural sector is mainly agriculture
1	the role and importance of the rural informal sector	mining developments do not employ many school leavers join informal sector growth and prosperity in informal sector will lead to other improvements
2	transport the biggest problem	roads, air, sea hard to transport goods to and from rural areas
3	high operating costs	caused by bad roads prevents expansion of informal sector
4	services	rural informal sector not getting support
5	law and order	theft of produce theft of store goods
conclusion	formal sector needed for future good economy	mines and large projects also have role

Student Book Chapter 3

Activity 8: Explaining how to do something

1. Over a period of time, collect hair of your own or family members.
2. Tie cane together with lianas in the shape of the wig.
3. Sew the lengths of hair to the frame using a needle made from flying fox bones and thread made from bark.
4. Melt some gum from the kilt tree.
5. Spread the gum over the hair to make it hard.
6. Make the outside of the wig smooth.
7. Rub the outside of the wig with pig grease.
8. Paint the wig in bright colours.
9. You can put on extra decoration such as scarab beetles.

Student Book Chapter 4

Activity 1: What is an 'idiom'?

He is the black sheep of the family,—the one who does not fit in with the rest

Never missing a golden opportunity—a very good chance

To take the lion's share,—take more than your share, more than everyone else

And build castles in the air.—to dream and for things than probably won't happen

He always has an axe to grind,—to do something for a selfish or wrong reason

And throws his weight around,—to be bossy

But he can not read between the lines,—can't see what is behind words or ideas

When dressed up to the nines.—dressed in fancy clothes.

Activity 5: What are similes?

1. She was as sweet as	honey.
2. His voice was as clear as	a bell.
3. Float like	a butterfly.
4. and sting like	a bee.
5. Her heart was as hard as	a stone.
6. They played as quietly as	mice.
7. He ran like	the wind.
8. The lake shone like	a mirror.
9. He stood up as straight as	an arrow.
10. He took to the new game like	a duck to water.

Activity 7: Questions about the passage

1. The children flew out of the classroom like birds from a cage. Children escaping, birds escaping (both getting away as quickly as they can)
2. It hit their shoulders like heavy fists. Strong wind, heavy fists (both like someone hitting your shoulders)

3. It fell like buckets of water being thrown sideways into their faces. Heavy rain, thrown water (both will really wet the children)
4. They looked like drowned rats by the time they reached shelter. Wet children, wet rats (both wet, hair wet)
5. The fire inside the house was as welcoming as a warm hug. Warm fire, warm hug (both welcoming)

Activity 9: Match the meanings

Colloquialism	*Meaning*
in the same boat	in the same situation
hard up	short of money
lion-hearted	very brave
thick in the head	stupid
stuck up	too proud
heavy-eyed	sleepy
play with fire	take risks
sit on the fence	not take sides
pull the leg	trick
put your foot in it	cause embarrassment

Activity 11: Questions about the passage

1. 8
2. Nothing
3. The woman said she thought the conversation had been most interesting.
4. No, except that he might have enjoyed it for its silliness and how he could use it when writing his books.
5. What a waste of time.
6. The conversation was not really a conversation. Nothing that was said made sense.

Activity 13: Questions about the language

- Swayed, gleamed, swished
- Quick movements
- All the things she values, perhaps a baby
- Winter
- Icicle, frozen
- Blood nipp'd—cold like a pinch on your skin; way foul—difficult to move around and do work; the three characters worked hard, even when it was very cold

Activity 14: Using word pictures

The day is done and the darkness
Falls from the wings of Night.
As a feather is wafted downward
From an eagle in his flight.

I see the lights of the village
Gleam through the rain and mist,
And a feeling of sadness comes over me
And my soul cannot resist.

Activity 15: Questions about the poem

1. Wings
2. No
3. Wafted—a slow movement
4. Birds, softness, lightness, how a feather floats slowly to the ground
5. No, the mist and the rain would hide all except the lights
6. A kind of pleasant sadness

Activity 17: Questions about the passage

1. To carry things from place to place
2. An animal used for carrying loads, for example, horse, bullock
3. They will keep on working until they die
4. Trudge, crouched, totter,
5. Day and year stress the repetitiveness of the life the writer is writing about, pattern stresses how the picture at the beginning of the passage has changed by the end.
6. Candle extinguisher, camel

Activity 18: How the choice of language affects the audience

A writer chooses his language for a purpose. The words a writer chooses can have an effect on us and make us react in certain ways.

1. Feel that they have a reasonable, happy life
2. E.g., at the beating heart
3. Student's own answer needed.
4. Should react with concern and sympathy
5. Yes, he feels very sorry. However, he realises he is a guest in another country and cannot change the way things are done.
6. Student's own answer needed.

Student Book Chapter 5

Activity 2: Answer these questions

1. The events in the story 'Jack and the Beanstalk'
2. A fairy tale
3. In the fairy tale the giant is killed. In the letters he is still alive and we hear how other people felt.
4. a) objection to this being a job for a young boy;
b) trying to get something good from what happened;
c) environmental protest;
d) looking for reward or compensation;
e) correcting the report; f) appealing for justice; g) trying to make money from the event.
5. a) negative; b) positive, hopeful; c) negative, looking beyond the event itself; d) hopeful, greedy; e) angry and upset; f) angry; g) greedy.
6. For example, for the giant or his wife.
7. Students' own answers needed.
8. Yes

Activity 4: Answer these questions

1. School
2. They could have been, George might have got the idea from that or just from nowhere
3. She was beginning to realise what was in the box and thinking it was a finger
4. Yes
5. She must have done so because they set up the joke against George
6. Yes
7. Threw up at the thought of eating a cat killed on the road
8. Students' own answers needed.

Activity 6: Answer these questions

1. Yes
2. That there must be a leak
3. Yes
4. Because they chewed a lot more gum than they were used to doing
5. It no longer seemed like a special treat
6. Chew more gum, find something else to block the hole, leave the car and catch a PMV??
7. Yes, the feeling is positive despite the problem
8. The family were together, doing things together, the problem was solved

Activity 8: Answer these questions

1. No
2. No
3. To sit around and let others do everything for you
4. Yes
5. When it was still happening the next morning
6. Some of them
7. No
8. Probably

Student Book Chapter 6

Activity 3: The main points

Fill in this table for the article on neem trees.

Paragraph	*Main topic of paragraph*	*supporting details*
1	origin of neem	India 1000s of years use against insects
2	spread to the world	1950 scientists observed locusts did not eat neem leaves scientists found the chemical that repels insects
3	introduction to PNG	by missionaries grows up to 800 metres above sea level
4	growth habits of neem	6 metres up to 20 metres tall
5	planting and care of neem	plant fresh seed prune for more leaves

Activity 5: Questions to help you find out information

1. Local Level Government
2. What is the name of the LLG in your area?
3. Council Chamber location
4. Varies, average 3, about 3.284 (1997) in PNG, with 5 747 wards
5. The President
6. The ward councillors
7. Urban wards have one appointed member, rural wards have two appointed members. Other women may be elected or represent other organisations with appointed members.
8. To represent people living in villages and settlements, pass laws, prepare plans and budgets, make sure services are delivered, and raise revenue.

Activity 7: Try some scanning

1. The student will look for a place name.
2. The student will look for the name of a river.
3. The student will look for a name.
4. The student will look for a Province name.
5. The student will look for a date.
6. The student will look for a number.
7. The student will look for a mountain name.
8. The student will look for an airport name.
9. The student will look for a number (in tonnes).
10. The student will look for the date 1975 and a name.

Activity 10: Answer these questions

1. Their parents
2. Informal

3. As a shoe mender
4. K30 to K40
5. Soap, firewood, kerosene and food
6. Village
7. City authorities
8. Honest

Student Book Chapter 7

Activity 2: Vocabulary activity

kuia	grandmother
mokapuna	grandchild
awhi	comfort
kai	food
karanga	call to important visitors
marae	area in front of the meeting house
Haere mai	welcome
mana	pride

Activity 4: Vocabulary activity

apart	standing alone
opportunity	a chance to do something
generous	giving freely
harvest	time when crops are picked
chatted	talked abut unimportant things
shortly	soon
I had no idea	I did not know about it.
urgent normal	something that needs to be done at once just the same as always
back and forth	to go in one direction and then the other direction
dismayed	feeling upset and unhappy
hurried	fast moving

Activity 15: The poet's way

1. Yes
2. A list with commas, no space between words, a / between words.
3. Yes, e.g., naked road
4. No—he does not have a capital letter at the beginning of each line.
5. Yes 'voice of birds' for birdsong and 'grey-haired wisdom' for age.
6. Yes, e.g., 'impartial lava'.

Student Book Chapter 8

Activity 2: Who is the audience, what is the purpose?

1. Informal (some students may think it is formal because it is factual, but the style is informal)
2. Language style
3. Colloquial
4. To make the reader feel personally involved in the topic
5. Young people
6. Mostly to entertain, does give some facts

Activity 3: Vocabulary activity

bossy	commanding
picked on	treated unfairly
scrounge around	beg for food or steal food
in each other's way	interfere with each other
run into	meet
from time to time	occasionally
break into a run	suddenly start moving
pretty much	mostly
goes on	continues

Activity 5: Who is the audience, what is the purpose?

1. Yes
2. Yes—to entertain
3. There are some facts, but these are not real cats, they are fantasy animals
4. Yes, students should get some fun out of it

5., 6., 7. Informal, italic and underlined words as above

8. Audience could be children or adults

Activity 7: Who is the audience, what is the purpose?

1. Yes
2. Yes, to entertain
3. Yes; these are real cats
4. 4, 5, 6, 7 and 8 as above

Activity 9: Comparing audience and purpose

1. The last one
2. *The Song of the Jellicles*
3. Yes, some in *Jellicles*, more in *Catalogue*
4. The articles are more written for a young audience, the poems are for a more general audience
5. The first three are mostly to entertain, the last article is to inform.

Activity 12: Questions about the article

1. No
2. No
3. The Christian perspective
4. Legalised revenge

5. Merciful, godly, just
6. Long-term imprisonment

Activity 14: How to read letters to the editor

1. a) elementary education is good, but should be for the rural areas; b) ANZAC Day and Remembrance Day should not be combined; c) stores are selling bad items; d) women should not wear men's clothing
2. a) not a failure; b) sadness, killing, rounded up, all they had done, lost generations, cheap labour, barrier, invasion, use our land as a battlefield, unjust, suffered; c) to make matters worse, shameful, cheating, exploit; d) daunim narapela poroman, nogat se, kisim trabel
3. a) more suited there as a common mother tongue is used (*not always*), not a failure, the only way our cultural identity will survive (*there are other ways*); b) ANZACs reflect with pride (*not all do*), all they had done was to run away and hide (*some may have taken a more active part*); c) these businesses are cheating us with counterfeit goods to exploit our limited resources (*some may be genuinely unaware that the goods are faulty*); d) Yupela ol meri laik kamap moa na moa yet olsem yupela save werim samting bilong ol man (*some may wear such clothes for other reasons*), Yupela yet save kisim trabel kam long yupela yet na bihain komplen kam bek long yumi ol man (*possible in some cases, but not all*)
4. a) 80%; b) compensation; c) poor condition of goods, no refund; d) wearing men's clothes

Activity 17: What do you think?

1. No, they both want you to believe them
2. Yes, the Minister says PNG E-FF is holding back development, PNG E-FF calls the development 'giaman'
3. Yes, for example: *Forestry brings much needed money, and social and economic development to PNG*; *The bridges break and building stand empty…*
4. PNG E-FF
5. students' own answers needed—*no,* because it makes you suspicious they are exaggerating; *yes,* because it makes you see clearly what the problem is.

Student Book Chapter 9

Activity 2: Questions about the poem

1. Yes
2. It appears that his memories are mostly happy
3. Gone, friends have died before him
4. Old and brown (dull, burnt out)
5. Yes
6. No, he has accepted that the end of his life is near

Activity 4: Questions about the poem

1. On surface (literally) life cycle of caterpillar, figuratively death and renewal perhaps
2. Hurry; walk (seem to contrast)
3. Being eaten
4. Cocoon
5. No

Activity 6: Questions about the story

1. No, he was using it as a farm vehicle
2. Someone offered him a lot of money
3. Because he only wants to drive that car
4. No
5. Yes

Activity 12: Questions about the play

1. Students may or may not believe him, he could just be doing the praying to stop his wife nagging.
2. They seem to be using it for themselves, no mention of charity as you would expect a gift from God to be used for (note: this is not the Christian God).
3. It seems that he knows what will happen when he talks about his poor clothes—he does plan what he is going to say to the magistrate and seems to have set it up beforehand.
4. Students may or may not believe he is honest. He must know that the gold was the moneylender's and he certainly knows that the coat and jewels are, so he is not being honest.

Activity 13: How to write plays

1. The way the writing is set out (format) with dialogue next to the name of the person who speaks it.
2. These are stage directions to tell the actors how to say something *(getting angry)* or where to go *(stepping aside)*.
3. This is telling the actor to say the word with stress, such as more loudly.
4. 'Props' is an abbreviation for properties, or the things needed for the play.
5. Stage setting is how the props and scenery are arranged on the stage.
6. The list of characters is at the beginning.

Student Book Chapter 10

Activity 1: Making your pronouns clear

There are several possible ways to correct most sentences. Students should pick the most likely way.

a. Hannah shouted when she called her sister. OR When she called her sister, Hannah shouted. OR To call her sister, Hannah shouted. OR Her sister shouted when Hannah called her.
b. Tau had a good time when he brought his cousin on the fishing trip. OR His cousin had a good time when Tau brought him on the fishing trip.
c. 'You are going bald,' Gabi told his father. OR Gabi told his father that he (the father) was going bald. (the most likely)
d. The dish broke when I put it in the bucket. (the most likely)
e. The A and B teams played a long game of volley ball, but in the end the A team won.

f. Strong chemicals should be locked in a cupboard to keep them away from children.
g. Kafa told Mubi that he (Kafa) had won the election. OR dialogue
h. Safira told Luci that the headmaster had asked to see her (Luci). OR dialogue
i. When Agata married, her mother went to Lae.
j. Manuia was a student when he first met Poro.

Activity 2: Dialogue writing

'Hi, Gemo,' said Sibona. 'Long time.'

'Hi, Sibona. Yes it's ages. What have you been up to?'

'Oh, this and that. Nothing special. Though I have a new job. Good thing, too. I was getting tired of living from hand to mouth.'

'Great. What is it?'

'Well, I don't want to let the cat out of the bag, as I haven't signed up yet. But I'm on to a good thing.'

'I'm pleased for you Sibona. Sounds like it is a real feather in your cap.'

'Yes, thanks. I've got to shoot through, now…so…catch.'

Activity 7: Metaphors

The bats are broken umbrellas hanging in trees (bats and broken umbrellas)

Til sunset they flap in a river across the sky (a lot of bats flying and a river)

Black on red

Into the gardens.

The noise of their wings are feet running (the sound of bats wings and the sound of running feet)

From the scene of a crime.

Your sharp teeth are chisels chipping at my sleep, (sharp teeth and chisels)

Your darkness is superstition, the colour of nightmares. (darkness and superstitions)

Activity 8: Match the metaphor

A garden hose is a snake in the grass

The moon a twenty toea coin

A back hoe machine is a dinosaur

A mosquito is a Red Cross nurse

The sun is a leaping fire

Rain is a shimmering scarf

An ant's nest is a bustling city

A mountain range is a backbone

Student Book Chapter 11

Activity 4: Read a poem with personification

Personification:

1. The book is standing—the comparison is with a person standing upright
2. Book has mouth—closed book compared with closed mouth
3. Book given emotions of loneliness and misery
4. Book is unmoving
5. Book is opened and speaks a story

Student Book Chapter 12

Activity 2: Talk about the article

1. Wantokism is being used wrongly and is hurting PNG.
2. Failing public service, failing public institutions
3. Yes, he feels it is dangerous.
4. They sound like facts but there is no proof given, e.g., *People are not happy about the very bad effects of crony-wantokism.*
5. Emotional, exaggerated, forceful
6. For example, evil, racist

Activity 4: Talk about the article

1. Women's issues need more media coverage.
2. Statistical study of articles over 6 months and impressions from interviews
3. Yes, that the coverage can be improved
4. Yes—statistics

Activity 7: Persuasion in advertising

1. Yes, the overall effect is to make you want the compu-phone
2. Students' choice
3. Before 1 July at the introductory price
4. Be part of [the future of communications]

Activity 12: Talk about the article

Writers use some persuasive devices to make their readers agree with their point of view.

1. In a rapidly globalising world this lack of unity puts PNG in a dangerous place.
2. For example: PNG remains a nation waiting to be built.
3. Students' point of view
4. Students' point of view
5. First and foremost
6. Their PNG identity comes a very distant last.
7. Our lack of unity leaves us open to other countries and multinational companies to come in and take over.
8. For example, take over, no effective [civil organisations], no sense of national purpose or national pride.
9. Audience: educated newspaper readers

Activity 15: Changing a persuasive passage

1. Should things other than food be sold at markets?
2. She feels they should not be sold.
3. Towards the end of the article
4. Take up too much space, appeal to children, break easily

Appendix 6: Glossary

Student Book Chapter 1

human rights these are the rights guaranteed under our Constitution and the United Nations, for example freedom of speech.

rural areas outside the towns

issue a point for discussion which is of general interest and about which people have differing points of view

discussion a form of conversation where a group of people talk together to solve a problem or to make their ideas clearer

persuasive language or actions which influence you to do something or to think about something

confident not shy, able to stand up and talk or read without getting scared

gesture a movement of the body, especially the hands, that means something to a group of people in general, a message which is not spoken

expression way of saying something, for example an angry voice expresses anger

tone way of saying something by using the voice to go up or down

argument a discussion about an issue with two sides, in which the speakers present their point of view about the issue

respond to listen, think about what was said and reply when you are having a discussion

situation where and when something happens

present to put on a performance or give a talk to others

statement a clear expression of a point of view

commentary a written discussion, usually showing a point of view

open-ended a type of question that allows the questioned person to give a longer answer that expresses feelings or point of view

Student Book Chapter 2

summarise find the main points and put them together in a paragraph

challenge decide to question the ideas

adapt change to suit what is happening

detailed using information to explain and giving examples

evidence facts that can be used

cause what makes something happen

reason what makes something happen

effect something that happens because of something else

result something that happens because of something else

signal a word that tells the reader what to expect

mime making ideas clear using no words, but facial expression and gesture

clarification making something clearer

refine getting rid of any rough parts, improving your writing

intonations different sounds

Student Book Chapter 3

form the genre, that is formal speech, play, prose reading etc.

purpose why the talking is being done

audience the expected people who will be listening to (or reading) the words

context where the people are, such as at a committee meeting, sitting around at the market

demonstration showing how something is done

speech map a diagram of how a speech is planned

framework a plan

develop add details to

chronological in order of time as events happen

organisational structures the form that is needed to help the reader follow a speech more easily, such as introduction

sophisticated oral language going a bit further in level of topic, words etc. than they did in Grade 6

Student Book Chapter 4

idiom a phrase that means something different from the words in it, used in informal language

cliché an overused word or idea

simile a way of comparing things using as or like, a poetic device

colloquial everyday speech

figures of speech clever use of language for a particular purpose, such as a simile

figurative language language that uses figures of speech and paints images or moods with words

react feel some kind of emotion as a result of what you hear or read

sympathy feel sorry for

empathy sharing another person's feelings

sensitive being aware of other people's feelings

Student Book Chapter 5

orientation setting up the beginning of a talk or story by telling who, what, where and why

build-up adding to, such as adding actions by cause and effect

complications problems which turn up along the way

pace how fast or how slow the story goes

resolution the solving of a problem or conflict

statistics figures which have been gathered using accepted means of research

factual texts texts which contain facts (objective texts)

literary text texts which are not necessarily all facts, but contain some imagination

fairy story an unlikely story with magical characters and events

preference something that you prefer for various reasons

action what the characters do

dialogue speech between two or more characters

description using adjectives, descriptive nouns or verbs to draw a verbal picture

diagram an illustration which shows how something is made or how something works

table grouping statistics under headings in columns

Student Book Chapter 6

style the various ways a writer can write; formal, informal, humorous, argumentatively

impersonal style detached from the reader, formal, objective

personal style involving the reader, informal, subjective

scan to look quickly over the surface of a passage to find a particular fact

scanning the action of looking quickly over the surface to find a particular fact

skim to look quickly over the surface of a passage to locate main ideas

skimming the action of looking quickly over the surface to locate main ideas

acknowledge to say or write where you got the facts and ideas that you have used

sources giving details of where you got the facts and ideas that you have used

Student Book Chapter 7

influence to cause to feel or act in a certain way

narrator the voice of the story

narrative the plot of the story or account

first person I, me (singular), we, us (plural)

third person he/him or she/her (singular), they, them (plural)

cultural identity what you believe makes you belong to a certain culture

attitudes ways of behaving and believing

image a picture

Student Book Chapter 8

match join things which belong together

contractions leaving out letters and joining two words together, such as they are ➤ they're

critically to look at carefully and think about the value of something

generalisation to make a general statement that talks about a group, such as Many people think that crime is increasing. Note: False generalisations make a claim about all of the group which applies to only part of the group: Everyone thinks crime is increasing.

personal things which concern you as a person, but may not be of general interest

emotive language language which expects an emotional reaction

repetition the act of repeating something, such as words, for a purpose

effective being successful in getting the effect you want

Student Book Chapter 9

reaction what happens when you are affected by something, you react. For example, your reaction to something very hot is to move away.

record write down in an orderly way

react what happens when you are affected by something. For example, you can react by crying if you are badly hurt.

personally belonging to you as an individual person, or someone else as an individual person

myth a magical story explaining an unknown fact or event, a non-scientific explanation, such as for why the moon changes shape

mythical belonging to myths

legend a story about a heroic man or woman, which may have become changed or exaggerated over the years

legendary belonging to legend

version another way of saying or writing something

conventions the accepted ways of doing something

Student Book Chapter 10

antecedent the noun or noun phrase that a pronoun replaces

ambiguous not clear in meaning, able to be understood in two different ways

pronoun a word used in the place of a noun or noun phrase to avoid repetition

refer go back to the noun or noun phrase

pronoun reference going back to the noun or noun phrases

metaphor a figurative comparison where one of the things being compared is said to be the other

metaphorical expression a way of saying something using metaphor

clarity without anything that can be misunderstood

clear without being able to be misunderstood

concise without extra, unnecessary words

conciseness the style of being clear without unnecessary words

refine to make more fine, better

direct speech as people speak, spoken dialogue with the correct punctuation

indirect speech someone's words given in a changed form and reported by someone else

handout a piece of writing given to go with a lesson, demonstration or speech which contains material relevant to the lesson etc.

practical demonstration to show how something is done using the real methods and ingredients

Student Book Chapter 11

figurative personal; poetic imagery

message the theme, the idea behind the story, the point of view held by the writer. For example, a story about a friendship between children of two groups that are opposed to each other could be giving the message that tolerance is good.

reconstruct to take something apart and then put it back together again in a different way

creative reconstruction to apply figurative language and new ideas

personification to give something human characteristics

mood the kind of feelings present in the writing

atmosphere the impression of mood and feelings that is given to the reader

meaning that which means something, something that matters, is not trivial

prose non-poetry

alternative a different but appropriate substitute

setting where, when, what mood a story takes place

Student Book Chapter 12

commentary a longer passage in which information and a point of view is given, a comment on relevant issue

focus article part of the newspaper where a commentary is given

evaluate to look at the successful and less successful aspects of something

quality the appropriateness of something, for example, are the facts correct and from a source you accept?

slogan phrase used in an advertisement that the readers/listeners are meant to remember

superlatives comparison of adjectives the most of something such as most important/best

exaggeration using stronger words and phrases than is necessary to get the effect and reaction that the writer is looking for

claim a statement of the point of view, assertion

humour something funny or amusing

emotion feelings